Foreword

By Diana Blum MD

It's hard not to start wondering who gets to decide -
What is the value of human life?

      Moral injury as a practicing physician in the 2020's is nearly impossible to avoid. I, like most doctors in America, feel handcuffed by a sick care system that doesn't prioritize the needs of each individual patient we took an oath to care for. This breeds distrust, which only inhibits healing. Those ill are told to get in line at the algorithmic factory of "healthcare" to follow arbitrary protocols the "system" has determined is worth it for you to lead a healthier life, sadly, with limited regard to your actual well-being.

      This is how most clinicians felt before 2020 and when the pandemic hit, things only got worse for both physician and patient. Trust was further eroded as our threat and fear buttons became chronically activated and our natural survival instincts quickly went into overdrive. Our "feeling" brains took over and our "thinking" brains were sadly nowhere to be found; that is, after all, how we are wired when our survival is at stake.

D1736110

I quickly found myself on the front lines of a tragic moment in history, feeling demoralized from what I saw unfolding. As a clinical neurologist who focuses on the chronic management of Parkinson's Disease, helping patients make end of life decisions is not uncommon.

But for many of my patients, this suddenly became a soul-searching time - with most asking themselves –

"What is it that I value?"

That's how most of my "end of life" discussions usually begin and with COVID raging, I suddenly found myself having many more of these conversations. Not only with my patients, but within my family and friendship circles - cancer, loneliness, and unprocessed trauma, just to name a few topics that transcended political lines and united us human to human. I was trying to hold space for all of those who were counting on me to have answers but the more I listened and learned, the more filled with despair I felt.

You see, I am also a mom. And in 2020, I was a rather naive mom of two adolescent girls. As schools shut down and parents became part time teachers, I quickly learned that the dehumanization of life I was witnessing unravel as a physician, was also sadly being misguidedly taught in our K-12 schools. What's worse, I would soon come to learn that the negative unintended consequences this was having on the escalating mental health crisis our teens were experiencing, didn't seem to matter to those in charge.

In 2021, "identity" had already become the hottest new educational trend. Instead of helping kids build self-confidence, resilience, and grit, our schools pivoted towards a new approach: glorifying victimhood, emphasizing immutable characteristics, and pegging groups of people against each other through concepts like intersectionality, propagating resentment, and division.

I was ironically told that this new strategy was intended to address disparities and would help the school district achieve the equity goals it was seeking. I was told this is how we improve diversity and inclusion within our schools, but how this was going to be achieved by the means they were proposing still made no sense to me.

Learning that our educators have decided to remove personal agency from the new curriculum to accommodate a binary oppressor/oppressed lens for viewing our much more complex world, was frightening, especially for this Jewish refugee from the USSR and granddaughter of holocaust survivors. I understand how quickly this type of teaching can turn to violence; my family was living proof. I embarked on a mission to find solutions and that was when I came across Empowered Humanity Theory.

I reached out to Jason, and we instantaneously connected as fellow humanity healers. His work in the classroom paralleled mine in the exam room. One of the ways I help my patients is teaching them how to recognize the intricate interplay between our emotions, our bodies, and our subsequent behaviors. Identifying unhealed emotional wounds, often by listening to signals the body is giving, we can tend to feelings of discomfort before they are heightened into more troublesome pain. This empowers us to make choices that can ultimately minimize our suffering.

When the human threat response has already been triggered (deadly virus, lockdowns, etc..) people's tribal reflexes kick in and we are primed for an even more amplified reaction as both brain and body are now on full alert. Evolutionary biology and cognitive neuroscience could have predicted what we observed in the aftermath of George Floyd. One of the most basic lessons in Cognitive Neuroscience is that "neurons that fire together, wire together". That is why exercise is so important in the management of Parkinson's Disease. The more you practice balance training exercises, the better your balance becomes.

Similarly, for optimal well-being, adopting a practice of self-compassion helps develop innate compassion for others. This promotes love and hope for a better society. Forced utopia can only be achieved through violence, and that must never be justified in a civilized world that prioritizes human dignity and life.

When fear and judgment are chronically perpetuated, then prejudice, aggression, and cruelty start to cloud life's precious beauties. This then leads to the abandonment of individual human dignity, at which point the value of life itself can be easily discounted. When the sanctity of life is destroyed, the natural progression is more hate and violence, ultimately culminating in atrocities, such as those witnessed on October 7th of this year (2023), the worst Jew slaughtering pogrom since the Holocaust.

So, what drew me to Jason's work? Most fundamentally, it encapsulates the meaningful solutions our chaotic world needs today. Rooted in cognitive neuroscience, Jason's value-based approach, cultivated in a dignity lens, using compassion and curiosity to address challenges resonated with me on both an intellectual and practical level. I was already incorporating all the same teachings in my clinical practice and seeing the remarkable results; thus, it was easy to appreciate how this work could further promote well-being in kids and society at large.

Doing the practice exercises outlined in this book fills my bucket of love and hope, the values I center along with kindness and compassion. If we have learned hate and helplessness by practicing habits that only sustain our unhappiness, then exercising the skills taught in Empowered Humanity Theory will cultivate the aptitude needed to rebuild trust and alleviate our suffering. May your healing begin....

Prologue

Around 2017, the growing mental health crisis, increasing societal division, and a surge in violence caught my attention. My concern for people and our future ignited a spark in me to find a widely embraced solution to build an empowering and dignified world. This compelling drive traces back to a sense of purpose instilled in me two decades ago during a late-night tragedy and fortified by my personal and professional experiences over the past twenty years.

More than a decade ago, I began telling my story without knowing the end and sharing an idea not yet fully formed in hopes of healing our divide and rehumanizing our culture and institutions. This path was arduous and painful, but in retrospect, those frustrations, moments of pain, and bouts of loneliness were necessary for concluding the story and solidifying the idea (Empowered Humanity Theory). These experiences provided me with the foundation to forge the attitudes and practices I now advocate for. While my story continued, the chapter I'd been trying to tell concluded, and the idea I had been trying to share solidified in the late summer of 2023. It is with gratitude and humility that I share my story and offer EHT to you as a framework for building an empowering and dignified life.

Sharing (what is now) EHT for the past six years has been an essential part of my sense of purpose. Examining my experience from 2003 onward, I find myself wondering if sharing EHT is my calling. The year 2003 marks a turning point because my life was inexplicably spared. This instilled a drive in me to live and pursue an intentional and meaningful life.

On December 21, 2003, I attended a wedding party, and upon leaving, an elevator malfunction provided me with a second chance at life. Instead of it opening on the 1st floor, it opened on the second. Nobody was waiting or in sight on the second floor, so I waited for the doors to close so that I could continue to the first. After nearly a minute, the doors remained open, and since I could see the stairs and my car from the elevator, I decided to take the stairs. This seemingly mundane delay would save my life less than twenty minutes later.

Later, down the road, I heard screeching tires and a loud crash and ultimately came upon spinning and smoking cars and horrific screams. A drunk driver was traveling in the wrong direction on the highway and collided head-on with the vehicle a minute or so ahead of me. In this car was a husband and wife with very young children, spending their first night out before their children were born. The wife was driving, and the husband was in the passenger seat. Their course of travel was nearly identical to mine, just a minute ahead.

The impact of the crash hit the passenger side, killing the husband and father upon impact. Had that elevator not malfunctioned, it would've been my sons who grew up without knowing their father. If I had been the fatality, my daughters would not have been born.
This experience etched a profound lesson into my being – never take life for granted, never settle, and relentlessly pursue what truly matters. It became the bedrock of a newfound attitude of living an intentional and meaningful life.

My elevator moment instilled in me a desire for a life infused with purpose; a life guided by love, hope, and adventure, devoid of regrets upon reflection. In 2011, I discerned that my life had veered into unpleasant territory: a strain in my marriage, professional discontent, and a desire to shield my young children (aged 4, 6, 8, 10) from a culture besieged by division, conflict, and chaos.

Embracing my second chance filled me with the courage to abandon the familiar for the unknown, to exchange a predictable and undesirable future for an opportunity to preserve my family by pursuing a joyful, less ordinary life. In 2012, I bid farewell to my role as a high school assistant principal and liquidated my assets – house, cars, and possessions – in pursuit of happiness abroad, with the vision of creating a Swiss Family Robinson-style adventure.

Our first stop was China, where I assumed the position of Director at a small K-12 International School. In a unique twist, I also scheduled myself as the PE teacher to share the school day with my children. This was initially intended as a two-year stint before relocating to a more remote, underdeveloped country.

However, within a few months, the "two-year commitment" was in doubt. I found myself in an interesting predicament. I was essentially a political football between the local government and my employing company. The outcome was the government's refusal to grant my family and me visas, coupled with the abrupt closure of the school.

This presented me with another unique opportunity. My employer offered to send my family and me back to the place we once called home or transfer us to Benin, Africa, where I would assume the role of Director at another school the following year. We opted for the latter, to continue our Swiss Family Littlefield Adventure.

While in Benin, my current sense of purpose was first breathed into me. Benin appeared to be the remote, underdeveloped Promised Land I envisioned. Unfortunately, my tenure in Benin also abruptly ended due to circumstances beyond my control. Several months into my assignment, the school signaled its intention to bring in another Director for the subsequent year.

Throughout my time in China and Benin, the strain in my marriage intensified, and now there was no other option but to return to Texas. The undesirable, predictable life I foresaw and worked to avoid was now likely my destiny.

Amidst this chaos, I found a moment of equanimity and first began to articulate the sense of purpose that guides me today. Initially discovering that we'd be leaving Benin, my mind raced, my heart pounded, and anxiety gripped me. Then, I remembered the elevator moment of 2003 and regarded this setback as another opportunity to start anew. I stilled my thoughts, focused on calming breaths, and voiced aloud what I refer to now as my Beninese Dream.

I posed the question to myself, "What do you truly want to do now, Jason?" My response was resolute, "I want to share my story with others, to inspire them to cultivate healthy mindsets, unlock their full potential, and increase the well-being of all people." Looking back, this is the precise moment I began the journey of developing EHT; I just didn't realize it at the time.

The years from 2014 to 2021 provided me with the professional expertise, personal suffering, and wisdom necessary to actualize my Beninese Dream. During those years, I worked as a Social Emotional Learning (SEL) Specialist. By 2016, my family unit split, and the undesirable outcome I had been evading and postponing was now my reality.

By 2017, I was settling into my new reality and began seeing hope in the situation and yet another opportunity for a fresh start. In retrospect, doing everything I possibly could to save what was important to me, losing it, and bouncing back from it was a process needed to tell my story and develop Empowered Humanity Theory. The personal suffering and recovering from it gave me the strength to endure a hostile work environment and bullying in the workplace from 2018-2021.

From 2017-2018, half of my working group participated in a professional learning group dubbed the "Equity Cohort". This workgroup received extensive training in the contemporary (and now institutionalized) framing of Diversity, Equity, and Inclusion (DEI) and antiracism. This new wave Civil Rights movement deviates from the theoretical underpinnings of past successful Civil Rights movements, which view individual liberties as fundamental and essential.

This new approach prioritizes group identities over individual liberties. It does so by absorbing individuals into group identity and assigning each group and all individuals labels of oppressors or oppressed. These labels are given based on the individual's inherent biological factors like skin color and sex. For a comprehensive critique of the dehumanizing contemporary practices, I recommend reading "The Lure of Disempowerment: Reclaiming Agency in the Age of CRT" by Matthew Abraham and Erec Smith.

By 2021, the new philosophy adopted by the Equity Cohort became the institutionalized expectation for the entire SEL department. 2021 was also the same year the newly imposed philosophy was adopted by CASEL, the national SEL organization as well as corporations and institutions worldwide.

Regardless of a person's intent, this newly adopted is disempowering, undignified, and dehumanizing to everyone because it unwittingly amplifies humankind's most primitive and barbaric traits and erodes groups' trust. When individuals view variations among people as less human than themselves, they amplify the in-group performance bias and innate propensities for prejudice, aggression, and cruelty.

Recognizing the unintended consequences of these new practices on psychological well-being, relationships, and society at large, I felt an urgent compulsion to chart a course forward that decreased our most barbaric impulses and applied our most benevolent.

In the summer of 2017, I began conceptualizing and shaping Empowered Humanity Theory. My earliest motivation was that I saw this as a framework my children could utilize for themselves and as a framework to make their world a better place. Since EHT pragmatically addresses the root cause of racism; I shared it with members of the equity cohort and was immediately met with hostility.

The dynamics of my close-knit circle of colleagues and friends took a sharp turn on the day I asked, "Can we discuss our approach to enhancing social-emotional well-being and addressing racism and inclusion?" Regrettably, over the next three years, my invitation to this conversation was never accepted.

Instead, over the ensuing three years, I found myself isolated and subjected to what is now commonly known as "cancel culture." When I announced my resignation, a colleague compassionately reached out, and told me, "It hurts my heart to see how you've been treated." I responded calmly, "I never took it personally; this is what the new ideology does and is partly purposed for."

This experience marked the inception of a value-centered identity. That is, individuals (me included) live a more robust and true-to-self life by operating from their chosen core values rather than assigned stereotypes. Integrity, dignity, and humor became the guiding principles that shaped my thoughts, actions, interactions with others, and even my perception of myself within this world. Integrity compelled me to confront uncomfortable truths about our society that will have far-reaching consequences for future generations. Dignity remained paramount, leading me to consistently attend to the well-being of my colleagues, guarding against further harm to our relationships. Upholding my dignity shielded me from internalizing the negativity bestowed on me by members of the equity cohort. My commitment to humor served as a tool for lighting the atmosphere, diffusing tense moments, and a way to provoke meaningful conversations.

13

In 2021, the SEL Specialist job description was rewritten to institutionalize the emerging contemporary DEI principles by creating a new position. Therefore, everyone in my department was required to reapply for their positions. This meant I could no longer simply do my job and question the dehumanizing attitudes and practices being perpetrated; advancing these dehumanizing attitudes and practices would not be the job itself.

In June 2021, I made one last attempt at dialogue by stating, "At its core, this new approach rejects human dignity and the principles of The Enlightenment." A colleague sternly replied, "It sounds like you want to go a different way than we do." This is when I leaned into my value of integrity heavily. I could take on this new role for job security and financial comfort or lean into integrity and cling to faith. I chose the latter.

I was as certain about my next move as I was when I discovered I would be leaving Benin, not sure but full of faith. I found myself drawn once again to embracing the unknown. This time, I refrained from expressing specific desires or hopes. Instead, I humbly extended my hands, palms up, and said, "Lord, my hands are yours; use them as you wish." With that, I left Austin for a rural community several hours away.

A few months after settling into my new Promised Land, life presented yet another jarring life challenge. In October 2021, my father moved in with me because his health began declining. I was his primary caregiver until his passing on March 26, 2023. In the wake of my father's death, I chose solitude. In my solitude, I came to the awareness that the story I was trying to tell and the idea I had been trying to articulate were now both complete and it was time to write and share both. My father's passing served as a poignant reminder of life's brevity and the importance of living a life infused with purpose and guided by love and hope.

Once again, I expressed gratitude for the seemingly random elevator moment, and the strength and wisdom acquired from 2017-2021, and began writing this book, which ultimately fulfilled my Beninese Dream.

My father was the grandest champion of my work and one of the earliest influences on it. Throughout my life, he often reminded me, "You gotta be more mindful, Jason." As a child, I didn't quite understand but into my adulthood, it made perfect sense to me. Therefore, in addition to this book serving as a guide to my children, it's also a memorial to my father.

Since 2017 I've established a value-centered identity, cultivated a dignity lens, and learned to prioritize mindsets of inquiry and compassion over fear and judgment so that I could better navigate the chaos, joys, and uncertainties of life. My only regret is not coming into this awareness sooner. While my experiences are unique to me, love, loss, grief, isolation, and joy are experienced by all. By intentionally cultivating what is best within us we can better navigate those moments.

This book serves as a guide to personal empowerment and dismantling the institutionalized dehumanizing systems that have taken root in post-2020 society. Reversing these trends in individual hearts, minds, and institutions is crucial for establishing an empowering and dignified society. For a compelling example of engaging with one another across racial lines with curiosity and compassion, I recommend reading "Letters in Black and White: A New Correspondence on Race in America" by Winkfield F. Twyman, Jr. and Jennifer Richmond.

Within the following pages, you will discover practical strategies, insights from neuroscience and philosophy, and a wealth of practices designed to help you cultivate a more empowered and dignified life. I encourage you to take these lessons to heart, reflect on your experiences, and integrate these principles into your daily life. Together, we can break down the dehumanizing attitudes, practices, and systems presently dividing us, nurture our well-being, and construct a society grounded in compassion and interconnectedness. The power for positive change resides within us all, and I invite you to join me in building an empowering and dignified world for all.

Chapter 1:
Introduction to
Empowered Humanity Theory

Beneath the complexities and specificities of our biology's and personalities, a profound truth resonates: all humans share an astonishing 99.9% of the same DNA. This shared genetic heritage binds us as members of the same human family. This awareness is fundamental to Empowered Humanity Theory (EHT). Building an empowered and dignified life begins with the understanding that all people are equipped with the capacities and propensities to harm each other as well as those that enable them to coexist in meaningful ways. When applied to daily routines and personal habits, Empowered Humanity Theory cultivates the latter.

Picture the human story as a grand tapestry meticulously woven with two essential sets of threads each embodying fundamental capacities and inclinations inherent in our human nature—encoded intricately in our DNA. One set of threads plays a pivotal role in preserving the tapestry against the storms, trials, and tribulations of our journey ensuring future generations can safeguard it and continue our shared narrative. The other thread set is designed to infuse comfort and beauty elevating our journey beyond mere survival. It's within the careful interlacing of these threads that we unveil our story.

Much like human emotions, responses, and motivations vary, so do the threads of our grand tapestry. The thread set designed to ensure durability is a sturdy, thick strand that can be woven with ease.

However, if weavers rely exclusively on this set, the tapestry loses its beauty aesthetics and comfort to the touch. Conversely, the thread set designed for comfort and beauty consists of finer threads demanding more time and deliberate effort for weaving. Over-reliance on this thread set renders the tapestry susceptible to holes and tearing. A skilled weaver not only selects the threads they use but also maintains a delicate balance between the two thread sets.

Both sets of threads are indispensable for human survival and the continuity of the narrative within the grand tapestry. However, they function more like the yin and yang, two opposites, rather than a harmonious duo working in tandem. For instance, the sturdy, thick, and easily woven threads represent the basic instincts of judgment, categorical thinking, in-group preference bias, and the capacities for prejudice, aggression, and cruelty (Zimbardo, 2007). This thread set equips us with the ability to make swift, life-saving decisions. Yet, when employed in non-life-threatening situations, these capacities can result in harm, limit our potential, and damage relationships.

In contrast, the finer, brighter, and more challenging-to-weave threads symbolize awareness, understanding, and compassion. These capacities not only contribute to our survival but also enrich and enhance our human experience, surpassing the benefits of prioritizing judgment, prejudice, aggression, and cruelty.

Together, these contrasting threads create a delicate balance in our human tapestry, providing us with both the swift responses needed for survival and the depth that makes our existence more meaningful and fulfilling.

Imagine that each quilted square represents an individual who has existed or is now living. Every addition to our human family is endowed with an empty square and an inexhaustible supply of both thread sets to tell their story, thus contributing to the rich narrative of our shared humanity. With awareness and intentional practice, we can prioritize the use of the finer threads while reserving the sturdier ones for mending immediate frays and tears. In doing so, our efforts are directed toward enhancing our personal experience and fortifying the interconnectedness between us.

Empowered Humanity Theory serves as a guiding framework leading each weaver to construct an empowering and dignified life while reinforcing our grand tapestry. Applying the principles of Empowered Humanity Theory in our daily routines and lifelong habits will steer us toward building an empowering and dignified future.

At its core EHT offers the proposition that humanity possesses an inherent capacity to shape a more harmonious world for present and future generations. The theory is built upon a foundation of developing and strengthening three specific attitudes by embedding 3 Pathways of Practice into daily routines and personal habits.

The Attitudes of Empowered Humanity Theory:

Value-centered Identity:
Developing an identity rooted in self-selected values allows for growth over a lifetime. Filtering life through chosen values aligns one's thinking, feeling, and behavior with their true self.

Dignity Lens:
Cultivating a perspective that places human dignity at the forefront of intrapersonal and relational interactions decreases the innate capacity for prejudice, and the propensity for categorical and dehumanizing thinking and strengthens trusting relationships.

Prioritizing Mindsets of Inquiry and Compassion:
Prioritizing attitudes of inquiry and compassion over those of fear and judgment allows for improved problem-solving and the easing of suffering.

The 3 Pathways of Practice
of Empowered Humanity Theory:

Practices that Build Awareness and Equanimity:

These practices promote insight into ourselves, each other, and the world around us. Mindfulness is a practice that builds awareness and equanimity enabling us to find calm during moments of chaos.

Practices that Build Kindness and Compassion for Self and Others:

These practices encompass encouraging and positive gestures, words, and acts of service extended without intentions or expectations. They also involve acknowledging and actively seeking to alleviate suffering whether it's one's own or another's.

Practices that Celebrate Our Common Humanity:

These practices highlight the similarities between people. Sharing stories and identifying elements of oneself within others are examples of practices that celebrate our common humanity.

Empowered Humanity Theory is grounded in the principles of neuroscience, human psychology, and evolutionary biology. It wholeheartedly embraces the concept of neuroplasticity acknowledging that our brain's architecture adapts to what we consistently practice.

By deliberately adopting attitudes and practices that elevate well-being and interconnectedness we interweave the fine threads of care, beauty, and compassion. Over time, the intertwining of these fine threads will create a bond even stronger than the thread set purposed for durability.

In the following chapters, the rich tapestry of EHT will be carefully unwound. Each thread will be meticulously examined and woven into a narrative that guides readers toward a deeper understanding of the theory's essence. As we embark on this journey together the subtleties of EHT's attitudes and practices will be unveiled, offering a roadmap not only for personal growth but also for the advancement of humankind toward an empowered and dignified future.

Chapter 2:

The Neuroscience of Wellbeing - A Foundation for Empowered Humanity Theory

Understanding the Intricacies of the Brain: A Guide to Empowerment

In this chapter, we embark on a journey to comprehend the intricate workings of the human brain. This knowledge serves as our guiding compass as we navigate the complex landscape of thoughts, emotions, and actions. We'll explore how this understanding can empower us to lead more dignified and empowered lives.

The Two Sides of the Brain: A Symphony of Functions

The brain is often compared to the conductor of a symphony orchestra, overseeing a performance that involves thoughts, emotions, and behaviors. Visualize it as a collaboration between two distinct hemispheres, each contributing its unique talents to the grand performance.

The left hemisphere excels in linguistic abilities, logic, and analytical thinking. It provides the intellectual scaffolding for grasping complex ideas, problem-solving, and constructing coherent narratives.

In contrast, the right hemisphere takes on the role of the creative maestro, specializing in spatial awareness and emotional processing. It sees the bigger picture, enabling us to interpret emotions, recognize patterns, and navigate three-dimensional spaces. This harmonious interplay between the hemispheres creates the rhythm of our cognitive experience (Referenced from "The Master and His Emissary: The Divided Brain and the Making of the Western World" by Iain McGilchrist).

Navigating Life's Currents

To illustrate our life's journey, we use the metaphor of the "River of Wellbeing," conceptualized by Dr. Daniel Siegel and Dr. Tina Bryson. Envision yourself in a canoe, navigating the twists and turns of this metaphorical river. Staying close to the center represents a balanced and harmonious existence. Yet, as life's currents push and pull us, our canoes often veer toward the banks of chaos or rigidity.

By embracing Empowered Humanity Theory (EHT), we equip ourselves with the metaphorical "paddles" necessary to steer our canoes back to the center. EHT practices help us maintain equilibrium, even in the face of unpredictable life currents. Through this metaphor, we recognize that an empowered and dignified life results from our ability to recalibrate and ensure our canoes remain steadily on the path to the heart of the "River of Wellbeing."

Integrating the Brain for Resilience and Balance

Research from The Human Connectome Project unveils a profound insight: psychological well-being thrives in an integrated brain. Picture the brain's hemispheres, circuits, and neural pathways communicating seamlessly, much like a synchronized orchestra. An integrated brain is a predictor of our ability to respond adaptively to life's challenges and uncertainties (Referenced from "The Developing Mind: How Relationships and the Brain Interact to Shape Who We Are" by Daniel J. Siegel, 2012).

However, just as a skilled conductor guides the orchestra to harmonious melodies, we too must learn to guide our brain's symphony. EHT's attitudes and practices emerge as the conductor's baton, orchestrating the harmonious interplay between our brain's components. By cultivating the practices of EHT, we learn to keep our metaphorical "canoes" consistently aligned with the center of the "River of Wellbeing."

The Amygdala, Hippocampus, and Prefrontal Cortex: Navigating Emotional Terrain

Our journey through the "River of Wellbeing" involves navigating emotional landscapes that often shape our decisions and actions. In this context, the amygdala, hippocampus, and prefrontal cortex play pivotal roles in our responses. Understanding these brain regions empowers us to harness their functions more effectively.

The amygdala, a small almond-shaped structure nestled within the temporal lobe, serves as the sentinel of emotions, particularly fear and anxiety. When activated, the amygdala ignites the body's stress response, leading to increased heart rate, rapid breathing, and perspiration. These reactions, remnants of our evolutionary past, aimed to keep our ancestors safe from imminent dangers like predators or rival tribes. In modern times, however, this primitive alarm system can often be triggered by mundane, non-life-threatening events such as social media interactions or traffic congestion (Referenced from "Emotion Regulation: Conceptual and Practical Issues" edited by Adrian Wells).

On the other side of the cognitive spectrum lies the hippocampus, a modest yet vital component responsible for memory formation and recall. Within its curved structure, short-term memories transform into lasting impressions, a process essential for learning and personal growth. The hippocampus also contributes to spatial navigation, guiding us through the physical world.

Nestled at the front of the brain, the prefrontal cortex acts as the conductor, regulating behavior, emotions, and executive functions like decision-making and problem-solving. It serves as the brain's control center, tempering impulsive reactions and enabling us to envision the long-term consequences of our actions.

However, when the amygdala rings its alarm bell in the presence of fear, it often drowns out the prefrontal cortex's rational voice. This is why fear-driven decisions tend to be reactive, disempowering, and sometimes undignified. EHT's practices encourage us to relegate fear and judgment to appropriate contexts, allowing us to cultivate emotional regulation, make empowered decisions, and build stronger relationships.

Navigating the Rapids of Stress

Stress, as depicted in "Why Zebras Don't Get Ulcers: An Updated Guide to Stress, Stress-Related Diseases, and Coping" by Robert M. Sapolsky, can be likened to the turbulent rapids of a river. In this analogy, it can either propel us forward like a skillful canoeist or capsize our canoes.

Brief moments of stress act like invigorating surges, providing the energy needed to perform under pressure. However, when stress becomes chronic, it's comparable to relentless rapids that relentlessly erode our overall well-being and brain health. This ongoing stress takes a toll on key brain regions, including the amygdala, hippocampus, and prefrontal cortex, steering our metaphorical "canoes" toward the banks of chaos or rigidity.

This issue is prevalent today. Recent surveys conducted by the American Psychological Association in 2022 underscore the extent of the problem. Nearly 27% of surveyed adults reported experiencing such high-stress levels that it significantly impairs their ability to function. This percentage skyrockets to 46% among adults under the age of 35, highlighting the widespread nature of this challenge.

EHT offers a lifeline in these turbulent waters. By embracing EHT's attitudes and practices, we enhance brain connectivity and transform our responses to stress. The result is a heightened ability to navigate these currents without compromising our empowerment or dignity.

Cultivating Well-Being

Ritchie Davidson's research adds another layer to the symphony of well-being. Through his work, we learn that well-being is a skill that can be developed and strengthened through intentional practices (Referenced from "The Emotional Life of Your Brain: How Its Unique Patterns Affect the Way You Think, Feel, and Live - and How You Can Change Them" by Richard J. Davidson and Sharon Begley).

This concept of neuroplasticity, the brain's ability to change based on what we practice and engage with, opens a world of possibilities. Just as a musician hones their craft through diligent practice, we can cultivate well-being through intentional engagement with attitudes and behaviors that promote resilience, outlook, attention, and generosity. EHT's attitudes and practices align seamlessly with Davidson's findings, offering a comprehensive framework for fostering well-being.

Orchestrating Empowerment through Brain Awareness

Unlocking the potential of our minds requires an understanding of its intricate workings. By recognizing the distinct functions of each hemisphere, navigating the emotional terrain with the amygdala, hippocampus, and prefrontal cortex, and managing stress through EHT practices, we chart a course toward empowerment and dignity. Just as a conductor guides an orchestra to a harmonious crescendo, we can conduct the symphony of our own lives, embracing EHT as our guiding baton. By doing so, we harmonize our brain's components, cultivate resilience, and establish a foundation for a life of empowerment and well-being.

Chapter 3:
Developing a Value-Centered Identity with Practices That Build Awareness and Equanimity

At the core of Empowered Humanity Theory (EHT) lies a foundational attitude — a value-centered identity. This attitude beckons us to transform how we perceive ourselves and the world around us, inviting us to transcend the limited, stereotyped, and biased identity markers used by modern societies.

In a world shaped by the contemporary DEI narrative, where individuals are pigeonholed into categories based on inescapable stereotyped traits, EHT offers a holistic identity framework that revolves around self-selected core values. A value-centered identity defies the notion that our identity should be predetermined by our innate biology. Instead, it champions the idea that our identity, the person we are, is rooted in the values that resonate personally. A value-centered identity fosters a deeper connection to our human experience than the contemporary DEI narrative.

The process of adopting a value-centered identity begins with introspection and reflection. Identify 3-10 core values that resonate deeply. (There's an activity to do so at the end of the Appendix.) These values serve as guiding stars, informing the way you perceive yourself and helping you navigate the stormy and calm seas of life. When faced with decisions or challenges, a value-centered identity prompts you to pause and ask fundamental questions: "Is my thinking aligned with my core values?" and "Is my behavior consistent with my core values?" This introspection offers a compass that guides your actions toward alignment with what you truly value.

What distinguishes a value-centered identity from other identity models is its dynamic nature. Unlike fixed identities, where individuals are confined to biological stereotypes and preconceived notions, EHT recognizes the fluidity of values over time. Life experiences, growth, and changing circumstances may lead to shifts in our value system. EHT invites us to recognize that our values may change over time, and that's perfectly natural. New situations may call us to lean more heavily into certain values, while periodic self-assessments can reveal the need for new values to emerge. This dynamic approach cultivates flexibility and adaptability, anchoring us in a state of constant growth while remaining true to ourselves.

Embracing a value-centered identity not only shapes our internal dialogue but also how we interact with and respond to others. A value-centered identity transforms our interactions, infusing them with a sense of authenticity and compassion. Instead of viewing others as stereotyped caricatures, we see them as fellow travelers on the journey of life, each guided by their own set of values.

Practices that Build Awareness and Equanimity

To strengthen the value-centered identity attitude, EHT suggests engaging in practices that build awareness and equanimity. These practices cultivate focused attention, emotional regulation, and a deeper understanding of self and others. By deliberately integrating these practices into our daily lives, we elevate our capacity for compassion, connection, and empowered decision-making.

1. Mindful Observation of the Environment

Start by engaging in the simple yet powerful practice of noticing your surroundings. Take a moment to pause and embrace the sights, sounds, smells, and textures that envelop you. Observe them as they are, without judging them as good or bad, pleasant or unpleasant. Be objective as you notice. This practice of mindful observation awakens your senses, grounding you in the present moment and heightening your awareness of the world.

2. Non-Judgmental Self-Observation:

Find a quiet space and turn your attention inward. Observe your thoughts, emotions, and physical sensations without judgment or reactivity. Observe your thoughts as if you are seeing balloons drift in the sky. This practice encourages you to cultivate self-awareness without allowing your inner critic to take control. Follow this self-observation with a series of focused breaths.

3. Reflective Journaling:

Embrace the practice of journaling to deepen self-awareness. Regularly dedicate time to reflect on your thoughts, experiences, and interactions. This practice provides a canvas for exploring the alignment of your behaviors with your chosen values.

4. Emotional Recognition and Vocalization:

In moments of heightened emotions, practice recognizing and vocalizing your feelings. Verbalize your emotions with statements like, "Right now, I am sad" or "Right now, I am angry." This conscious recognition of emotions integrates the brain's hemispheres, promoting emotional regulation and empowering you to navigate challenges from a centered space.

5. Mindfulness Practice:

Embrace the art of mindfulness—a practice that builds both awareness and equanimity. Mindfulness involves paying attention on purpose, in the present moment, and without judgment. By cultivating an open and accepting attitude toward thoughts, emotions, and sensations, you enhance your emotional regulation, reduce stress, improve focus, and increase your self-awareness.

Empowering Neurological Impact:

In recent years, mindfulness practice has gained widespread attention for its positive effects on emotional regulation and brain function (Lazar et al., 2011). Studies have shown that mindfulness practice can lead to increases in regional brain gray matter density, suggesting structural changes associated with enhanced cognitive functions (Lazar et al., 2011).

Additionally, research by Davidson et al. (2003) has demonstrated alterations in brain and immune function resulting from mindfulness meditation. Regular practice increases gray matter density in areas responsible for emotional regulation, memory, and learning. It reduces activity in the brain's default mode network, associated with self-referential thinking. These findings indicate the profound impact of mindfulness (a practice that builds awareness and equanimity) on our neural pathways and emotional well-being.

Equanimity and Emotional Balance:

The equanimity cultivated through mindfulness promotes calmness, composure, and emotional balance, even in the face of chaos. By observing moments with objectivity rather than judgment,
you prevent the amygdala from hijacking higher-order thinking during crucial situations, fostering empowered decision-making.

The Evolution of Identity:

A value-centered identity thrives on the recognition that values change over time. Allow for the evolution of your values as you grow and learn from life's experiences. Embrace the flexibility to adjust your values based on emerging insights and shifts in your life journey.

Incorporating these practices into your daily life enhances your ability to regulate emotions, retain focus, and make empowered decisions. By building awareness and equanimity, you lay a strong foundation for a dignified life that's aligned with your core values.

These practices bridge the gap between theory and lived experience, allowing you to steer your canoe back toward the middle of the "River of Wellbeing" during moments of chaos or rigidity.

As philosopher William James insightfully observed over a century ago, the ability to consistently refocus wandering attention is central to judgment, character, and will. Empowered Humanity Theory offers a pathway to this ideal — a practical means of cultivating awareness and equanimity. By nurturing these qualities within us, we pave the way for an empowered brain, a more profound sense of interconnectedness, and a world that embraces the beauty of human diversity through the lens of shared values. As we navigate the journey toward empowerment, awareness, and unity, the Value-Centered Identity stands as a beacon, illuminating the path to a more dignified and empowered existence for ourselves, our communities, and society.

Chapter 4:
Cultivating A Dignity Lens With Practices That Celebrate Our Common Humanity

The Empowered Humanity Theory (EHT) Attitude — cultivating a dignity lens is the cornerstone for building a dignified community and society. This attitude transcends the boundaries of the contemporary narrative by fostering a profound understanding of our shared humanity. It promotes personal empowerment and paves the way for a peaceful society built on dignity and compassion. A dignity lens, as EHT envisions it, will transform how we perceive ourselves and others, setting the stage for dignified communities and society at large.

The Allergenic Response of "Othering":

Efferson, Lalive, and Fehr (2008) aptly observed that the moment we mentally exclude someone from our circle of "us," our minds subtly devalue that person and rationalize mistreatment. This automatic and subconscious response illustrates how humans have an allergic reaction to "othering," a process of perceiving someone as fundamentally different from themself. A dignity lens challenges this instinct to "other" by inviting us to consciously shift our focus toward our shared humanity rather than differences.

Human vs. Being:

Central to the concept of a dignity lens is distinguishing between the human and the being. *The human* is the sum of biological traits, outward personality, and the acquired skills that make each person distinct from one another. The latter refers to the innermost essence of all individuals. *The being* is characterized by two fundamental qualities: the desire to alleviate suffering within oneself and the aspiration to alleviate the suffering of others. Contemporary practices and attitudes' reliance on biological differences denies *the being* within all people. Shifting away from this standard will rehumanize our society in profound ways by removing the walls of indignities that the contemporary DEI narrative reinforces.

Dignity Violations and Empowered Communities:

In the pursuit of an empowering and dignified society, understanding the concept of dignity violations is important. Researcher Donna Hicks, Ph.D., contends that violations of dignity are the root of all harm. When individuals feel unheard, unseen, and unworthy, they tend to react with disempowering behaviors and coping mechanisms that often violate their dignity and/or the dignity of others. By cultivating a dignity lens, we strive daily to reduce the frequency and intensity of dignity violations within our communities.

Unveiling the Dignity Lens:

The initial step towards cultivating a dignity lens is recognizing that every individual possesses equal inherent worth and value of the highest regard. Embrace the notion that each person is a whole and unique human being that shares the same fundamental instincts and drives that you do. This way of human interaction stands in stark contrast to the reductionist practices of the contemporary, dehumanizing practices that pigeonhole individuals according to their inherent biological traits, thus reinforcing the innate human capacity for prejudice.

Shared Humanity and Universal Traits:

By celebrating our common humanity, we gain insight into the universal traits, desires, and motivations embedded in human nature. An empowered and dignified life entails reserving our primitive survival-based responses for situations of genuine threat. It means recognizing that all individuals yearn for social connection, possess a common pursuit of happiness, and exhibit compassion and curiosity. Cultivating a dignity lens strengthens our interconnectedness and curbs our innate capacities and responses that activate dignity violations.

Bridging Differences through a Dignity Lens:

Navigating life through a dignity lens means seeing the humanity in all individuals, bypassing the urge to categorize people according to assigned contemporary, normalized, and institutionalized practices, to cultivate the interconnectedness between yourself and others. This lens empowers us to focus on our commonalities, deconstructing walls of indignity constructed over time and preventing their reconstruction.

Practices Celebrating Our Common Humanity

Practices celebrating our common humanity strengthen and reinforce our dignity lens. These practices acknowledge that all individuals seek belonging, form healthy bonds, and experience moments of loss and joy — much like you. This acknowledgment empowers us in ways that erode the walls of indignity maintained by the contemporary "identity" narratives that divide us from one another. Throughout each day, consciously view those who appear different from you as possessing qualities, motivations, and values similar to your own. Recognize your shared desire for belonging and pursuing meaningful life experiences.

Sharing Stories:

Actively listen to other's stories and seek aspects of yourself within their stories. Vulnerably share your experiences with others so they can find aspects of themselves that reside within you. Engage in conversations with family, coworkers, schoolmates, and strangers. Through shared stories and hobbies, create bonds that empower and dignify your community.

Building an Empowered and Dignified Society

Societies that wholeheartedly adopt a dignity lens relinquish dehumanizing practices. By shifting away from divisive models, communities will create a sense of belonging for all people and strengthen bonds between them. When a Dignity Lens guides behavior, the scourge of prejudice diminishes, making room for an environment free from biological-based prejudice.

By developing your dignity lens, you contribute to an empowering and dignified life for yourself and a world that honors our common humanity. As you partake in this transformative practice, envision the groups you belong to and how a dignity lens can amplify their purpose. As you build a dignified life for yourself, remember that you're simultaneously crafting a dignified world for all.

Chapter 5:

Prioritizing Mindsets of Inquiry and Compassion with Practices That Build Kindness and Compassion for Self and Others

The final EHT attitude for building an empowered and dignified life is — prioritizing mindsets of inquiry and compassion. This attitude serves as a beacon that guides us away from the pitfalls of prioritized mindsets based on judgment and fear. Prioritizing inquiry and compassion lead to a path of understanding, cooperation, and growth. The power of mindsets lies in their ability to shape our perceptions, interactions, and responses. They influence the lens through which we view experiences, relationships, and possibilities, ultimately determining the course of our lives.

Understanding the Power of Mindsets:

Our mindsets wield immense influence over our daily lives. They dictate how we interpret ourselves, others, and the world around us. From the goals we set to our reactions to adversity, our mindsets serve as the foundation upon which we build our experiences. They can either empower us to soar to new heights or shackle us with self-imposed limitations. Mindsets also construct the personal narrative that safeguards our physical well-being, guiding us toward decisions that mitigate potential risks.

For example, fear and judgment-based mindsets steer us toward the bank of chaos or the bank of rigidity. By prioritizing inquiry and compassion, we're better able to guide our canoe towards the center of the River of Wellbeing. In essence, mindsets constitute the building blocks of an empowered and dignified life, because they actively promote problem-solving and easing human suffering.

The Role of Mindsets of Fear and Judgment:

The EHT attitude of prioritizing mindsets of inquiry and compassion addresses our innate human tendency to prioritize mindsets fueled by fear and judgment. Evolutionary psychology has instilled in us a negativity bias. Our negativity bias amplifies our perception of "negative emotions" compared to "positive emotions." This bias once served the survival of our ancestors, protecting them from immediate and future threats. In the modern context, our negativity bias often leads to ruminating on doubt and criticism, ignoring the positive or spiraling into chaos or rigidity.

The fear and judgment spurred from our negativity bias can drive argumentation, limit personal potential, and even hinder others' growth as well. In shifting towards the EHT Attitude of Prioritizing Mindsets of Inquiry and Compassion, we chart a course away from the confines of our negativity bias, unlocking the potential for personal empowerment and a dignified society.

Developing the Attitude of Inquiry and Compassion:

Cultivating the EHT attitude of prioritizing mindsets of inquiry and compassion begins with the raised awareness of any fear of judgment-based thoughts that are limiting and critical. If no immediate danger is present, lean towards inquiry and compassion. This entails asking questions, seeking information, and exploring potential outcomes. Observe the moment for any possible underlying suffering that could be tended to. This attitude is developed over time by continuously disrupting thinking and decisions where fear and judgment limit your potential and the potential of others and or hinder relationships.

Evolving Through Inquiry and Compassion:

A fear and judgment-based mindset often arises from discomfort with present, past, or potential suffering. By viewing such moments through a compassionate lens, we can alleviate or prevent suffering and grow in areas of our choosing. In the face of challenging people and situations, our amygdala triggers a fear response, which can lead to harsh judgments and assumptions that separate us in chaotic and rigid ways. Responding with inquiry and compassion, in situations where physical safety is not at risk, offers an avenue for personal and mutual growth and an opportunity to ease any possible noticeable or underlying suffering. This consistent practice diminishes unnecessary amygdala responses, which is essential for building an empowering and dignified life.

Impact on Relationships and Empowerment:

The Attitude of Prioritizing Mindsets of Inquiry and Compassion aids in fostering deeper connections and enriches relationships. Compassion directed both inwards and outwards, reduces self-criticism and bolsters resilience when confronting challenges. By embracing inquiry and compassion, individuals become more apt to take calculated risks, explore novel opportunities, and challenge self-imposed limitations. Their approach becomes more creative, innovative, and assertive in pursuing their aspirations.

Moreover, this mindset has far-reaching effects on social interactions. It encourages constructive dialogue, active listening, and the pursuit of common ground. Instead of perpetuating division and conflict, prioritizing inquiry and compassion fuels cooperation and collaboration, nurturing a society where individuals thrive together.

Building Empowerment through Compassion and Kindness:

Integrating practices that build kindness and compassion for self and others strengthens the EHT attitude of prioritizing mindsets of inquiry and compassion. It's important to differentiate between kindness and compassion. Kindness involves simple acts of goodwill, while compassion demands a more profound engagement that involves tending to a moment of suffering.

EHT also emphasizes self-compassion, fostering self-kindness and compassion like what we extend to our friends. This practice enables us to learn from experiences without being trapped by self-blame or self-criticism, embracing our humanity with all its imperfections.

Impact on Psychological Well-being:

Engaging in these practices profoundly influences psychological well-being. Practices that build kindness and compassion swiftly impact the "outlook" and "generosity" components of well-being identified by Ritchie Davidson and The Center for Healthy Minds. By shifting our narratives from judgment and fear to inquiry and compassion, we open ourselves to positivity and generosity, which enhance our well-being. This transformation is immediate and lasting. This creates a ripple effect that resonates across interactions, relationships, and generations.

Creating a Dignified World:

Prioritizing Mindsets of Inquiry and Compassion is more than a personal practice—it's instrumental in building empowered lives and empowering societies. Setting aside harsh judgment and unnecessary fear fosters environments that embrace belonging and connectedness. The shift from divisive approaches to truly inclusive attitudes paves the way for nurturing the potential of all people by valuing every individual's journey.

As we incorporate this attitude into our lives, let's consider the groups we belong to and how embracing this mindset can elevate their purposes. By prioritizing inquiry and compassion over judgment and fear, we elevate ourselves and contribute to creating an empowered and dignified world for everyone.

Chapter 6:

Building an Empowered and Dignified Life

Empowerment is defined as "the process of becoming stronger and more confident, especially in controlling one's life and claiming one's rights". By recognizing the primitive thinking and behaviors we're all capable of and the root cause of our propensity to harm each other, we take greater control of our lives.

By navigating our experience with a value-centered identity with a dignity lens prioritizing mindsets of inquiry and compassion and incorporating practices that build awareness and equanimity. practices that celebrate our common humanity and practices that build kindness and compassion for self and others throughout daily routines in habits, we can not only take greater control of our lives, but we can thrive in our experience by building an empowering and dignified life for ourselves and our communities.

Developing these attitudes and engaging in the practices of Empowered Humanity Theory empower us by strengthening the neural circuitry linked to our psychological well-being and mitigating our primitive responses that cause relational damage, harm, and chaos. EHT's attitudes and practices are also consistent with multiple ancient teachings across cultures, people, and time.

The EHT theme of "We become what we practice" is reflected in a story that is often attributed to the Cherokee. It's a story about the two wolves inside of us. It begins with an elder teaching his grandson a life lesson about two wolves. He tells his grandson that inside each person, there is a constant battle between two wolves.

The first wolf represents negative qualities such as anger, envy, greed, resentment, ego, and arrogance. It embodies all the vices and destructive emotions that can lead to suffering and harm for oneself and others. This wolf also represents the behaviors linked to our most primitive self. This one is driven largely by fear and judgment and fluctuates between the banks of chaos and rigidity rather than the calm waters.

The second wolf represents positive qualities such as love, compassion, kindness, compassion, humility, forgiveness, and generosity. It embodies all the virtues and constructive emotions that bring joy, harmony, and well-being to oneself and others. This wolf also represents us as our best selves. A best self that is at peace with itself and connected to others and when thrown off course, sets and works towards an intention to get back to calmer waters. The grandson, intrigued by this teaching, asks his grandfather, "Which wolf will win?" The wise old Cherokee replies, "The one you feed."

The story serves as a metaphor for the ongoing internal struggle between our negative and positive tendencies and predispositions. It emphasizes the importance of cultivating and nurturing the positive qualities within us while recognizing and resisting negative influences.

Ultimately, the story teaches us that we have the power to choose which wolf we feed by the thoughts we entertain, the actions we take, and the values we uphold. By consciously focusing on the positive aspects and making choices aligned with love, compassion, and kindness, we can nurture the good wolf and create a more harmonious and fulfilling life for ourselves and those around us. Best Wishes-Jason

Appendix A
PRACTICES THAT BUILD AWARENESS AND EQUANIMITY

The following section contains multiple practices that build awareness and equanimity. Engaging in these practices helps develop the EHT attitude, value-centered identity. Explore all practices and return to the ones you find meaningful. This is not a comprehensive list as the number of possible practices is infinite. As you familiarize yourself with the practices named here, think about other possible practices that build awareness and equanimity you can authentically engage in.

Thinking about the positive impact these practices have regarding brain health and well-being combined with the neuroplasticity principle of "we become what we practice", consider adding the practices you find meaningful into your habits and routines to create an empowering and dignified life.

51

Value-Setting Exercise

Scan the list of values and make note of the ones that resonate with you. Distribute the list of values to each participant. Trust your instincts and choose values that genuinely resonate with your core beliefs and aspirations. No need to overthink and/or second-guess yourself. If a value that's important to you is not listed, add it/them to the provided list.

Accountability	Fidelity	Patience
Adaptability	Foresight	Peace
Altruism	Grace	Persistence
Ambition	Gratitude	Poise
Assertiveness	Growth	Purpose
Awareness	Happiness	Reverence
Balance	Hard Work	Security Self-
Bravery	Honesty	reliance
Calm	Honor	Serenity
Compassion	Hope	Service
Connection	Humility	Simplicity
Consciousness	Humor	Spirituality
Consistency	Imagination	Stewardship
Courage	Independence	Teamwork
Creativity	Insightful	Toughness
Curiosity	Inspiring	Trust
Dignity	Integrity	Truth
Empathy	Joy	Unity
Endurance	Kindness	Valor
Equality	Liberty	Vigor
Ethics .	Logic	Vision
Excellence	Love	Vitality
Fairness	Loyalty	Welcoming
Family	Openness	Wisdom
	Optimism	Wonder

After the initial scan and identifying, if there's a value you hold that isn't represented, feel free to add it to your list. Now edit the list down to the top 10 values that are most important to them. Consider the values that truly reflect who you are and what you want to embody in your life.

Now refine the list by selecting the top 5 values that hold the most significance to you. Reflect on the values that align closely with your sense of self and what you want to prioritize in your lives.

Finally, narrow this list down to the top 3 values that you consider the most essential to your core self. These values will serve as guiding principles in your thoughts, interactions, and habits.

Throughout your day ask yourself questions such as:
 "Are my thoughts aligned with my values?"
 "Are my interactions aligned with my values?"
 "Are my habits and routines aligned with my values?"
Adjust whenever necessary to ensure alignment.

Call to mind these values and what they mean to you during challenging and chaotic times. They can assist with providing clarity, motivation, and guidance when faced with difficult decisions or situations.

Core values can and will evolve over time, and it is essential to periodically reevaluate one's top values. Repeat the value-identifying process at regular intervals to ensure their values continue to align with your personal growth and aspirations.

Reflecting On Thoughts, Feelings, and Behaviors to Cultivate Awareness and Insight

Find a quiet and comfortable space: Find a quiet and comfortable space where you can be alone and focus on your thoughts and feelings without any distractions.

Set a timer: Set a timer for 10-15 minutes to give yourself enough time to complete this exercise.

Reflect on your thoughts: Start by reflecting on your thoughts. Pay attention to the thoughts that are going through your mind right now. Are they positive or negative? Are they related to a particular situation or experience?

Reflect on your feelings: Next, reflect on your feelings. How are you feeling right now? Are you feeling happy, sad, anxious, or stressed? Try to identify the specific emotions that you are experiencing.

Reflect on your behaviors: Finally, reflect on your behaviors. Think about how you are acting in response to your thoughts and feelings. Are you withdrawing, avoiding, or taking action? Are you engaging in any behaviors that are not in alignment with your values or goals?

Write it down: Take a few moments to write down your thoughts, feelings, and behaviors in a journal or on a piece of paper. Writing it down can help you process and organize your thoughts and gain more clarity.

Analyze and connect the dots: Once you have finished reflecting and writing, analyze your thoughts, feelings, and behaviors. Try to connect the dots between them and understand how they are related. For example, are your negative thoughts contributing to your feelings of anxiety, which in turn are causing you to withdraw from social situations?

Plan for improvement: Finally, use your newfound self-awareness and insight to plan for improvement. Think about what changes you can make to your thoughts, feelings, and behaviors to better align them with your values and goals. Set small, achievable goals that will help you make progress over time.

Exercise To Practice Assertiveness and Clear Communication

Identify a situation where you need to assert your needs clearly. It could be at work, in a social setting, or in a personal relationship.

Write down your needs in a clear and concise manner. Use "I" statements to express what you want, rather than blaming or accusing the other person. For example, "I need you to stop interrupting me when I'm speaking," instead of "You always interrupt me and it's really frustrating."

Practice saying your needs out loud. You can say them in front of a mirror, record yourself saying them, or practice with a friend or family member.

Imagine different scenarios in which the other person might respond to your needs. Think about how you might respond in each scenario, while still maintaining your assertiveness and clear communication.

Finally, role-play the situation with a friend or family member. Have them play the role of the other person and practice asserting your needs in a clear and assertive manner.

Remember, practicing assertiveness and clear communication takes time and effort, but the more you practice, the easier it will become. Good luck!

Focused Concentration Exercise

Find a quiet and comfortable place to sit or stand where you will not be disturbed. Take a few deep breaths and allow yourself to settle into the present moment.

Choose a nearby object to focus on.
Gaze at the object with a soft and steady gaze.
Take in as many details as possible, noticing the colors, shapes, textures, and patterns of the object.

If your mind begins to wander, simply bring your attention back to the object and its details. If thoughts arise, simply observe them without judgment and then gently guide your focus back to the object.

As you continue to focus on the object, imagine that you are breathing in its essence or energy. With each inhale, feel that you are taking in the qualities of the object, and with each exhale, imagine that you are releasing any distractions or mental clutter.

As you focus on the object, see if you can enter a state of "flow," where you become completely absorbed in the object and lose track of time.

When you're ready to come back, take a deep breath and slowly shift your focus back to the present moment. Take a moment to express gratitude for the opportunity to focus your attention and cultivate your concentration.

Exercise To Cultivate Gratitude

Find a quiet and comfortable space where you can sit or lie down without distractions. You may choose to keep a notebook and pen nearby if you'd like to write down your reflections.

Close your eyes and take a few deep breaths to relax and center yourself. Allow any tension or stress to melt away as you breathe deeply.

Begin by recalling three things or aspects of your life that you are grateful for. They can be simple or significant, personal or universal. Focus on the feeling of gratitude associated with each of these things.

As you reflect on each item, think about why you are grateful for it. Consider the positive impact it has had on your life, the joy or fulfillment it brings you, or the ways in which it enhances your overall well-being.

Engage your senses to deepen your gratitude. For each item, imagine the specific sights, sounds, smells, tastes, or physical sensations associated with it. Allow yourself to fully immerse yourself in the experience of gratitude for each aspect.

Take a moment to express your gratitude internally. Say "thank you" in your mind for each of the things you've identified. You can also visualize sending your gratitude out into the universe or directing it towards the people or circumstances that have contributed to your gratitude.

Expand your gratitude by thinking about other areas of your life that you appreciate. Consider your relationships, opportunities, accomplishments, or the natural world around you. Allow yourself to generate a sense of gratitude for the abundance in your life.

If you have chosen to keep a notebook, you can take a few minutes to write down your reflections. Jot down the things you are grateful for and any thoughts or feelings that arose during the exercise. This can serve as a reminder to revisit when you need a boost of gratitude in the future.

When you feel ready, gently bring your awareness back to the present moment. Take a few more deep breaths, wiggle your fingers and toes, and slowly open your eyes. Practicing this exercise regularly can help cultivate a mindset of gratitude and appreciation, leading to increased happiness and well-being. Remember to be patient and compassionate with yourself throughout the process.

Exercise For Identifying Personal Strengths

Begin by setting aside some quiet time for yourself, free from distractions. Grab a notebook and pen or open a new document on your computer.

Think back over your life and identify moments when you felt particularly proud, accomplished, or happy. These might be achievements in school or work, positive interactions with others, personal growth experiences, or any other moments that stand out to you.

For each of these moments, ask yourself what personal qualities or strengths you demonstrated in order to achieve or experience them. Did you show perseverance, creativity, leadership, kindness, or any other positive trait? Write down the specific strengths that come to mind.

Next, think about the feedback you've received from others. Have friends, family members, or colleagues ever commented on something they appreciate or admire about you? What do they typically rely on you for or seek you out for help with? Write down any recurring themes you notice.

Reflect on the strengths you've identified so far.
Are there any that stand out as being particularly important or meaningful to you? Circle or highlight these.
Finally, take a moment to consider how you can apply your identified strengths to your life moving forward. How can you leverage these qualities to achieve your goals, improve your relationships, or enhance your overall well-being? Write down any ideas or plans you come up with.

Exercise For Identifying Areas for Personal Growth

Set the Stage: Find a quiet and comfortable space where you won't be interrupted. Take a few deep breaths to center yourself and prepare for self-reflection.

Reflect on Core Values: Think about your core values and beliefs. Consider what truly matters to you in life, such as integrity, compassion, personal development, relationships, or any other values that resonate with you. Write down these values in your journal.

Emotions and Alignment: Review your list of core values and reflect on your current emotional state. Consider how well your life aligns with these values. Are you living in harmony with your core beliefs? Write down any emotions or thoughts that arise, whether positive or negative.

Identify Areas for Growth: Focus on each core value individually. For each value, ask yourself:
Are there areas in my life where I'm not living in alignment with this value?
What aspects of my life need improvement or growth to better reflect this value

Can I identify specific behaviors, habits, or thought patterns that are hindering my alignment with this value?"

Write your reflections for each value.

Prioritize Areas of Growth: After examining each core value, rank them in order of importance or urgency. Identify the areas where you believe personal growth is most needed based on your values.

Set Clear Intentions: For the top-priority areas, define clear intentions. Describe how you would like to grow or improve in these areas. Ensure these intentions are actionable, specific, and achievable. Consider what practical steps you can take to align your life more closely with your core values.

Develop Your Empowerment Plan: Create an empowerment plan based on your intentions. Outline the specific actions, milestones, or habits that will help you achieve your goals in the areas you've identified for growth. Ensure that your plan incorporates the principles of EHT, such as the value-centered identity, the dignity lens, and prioritizing mindsets of inquiry and compassion.

Practice Mindfulness: Spend a few minutes practicing mindfulness. Close your eyes, take deep breaths, and focus on the present moment. Reflect on the sense of empowerment that comes from acknowledging areas for personal growth and setting intentions to address them.

Journal Your Insights: Take time to summarize your insights from this exercise in your journal. Reflect on how EHT principles can guide you on your journey to personal growth. Express any feelings, thoughts, or realizations that emerged during the exercise.

Commit to Action: As you complete this exercise, make a commitment to yourself to take concrete steps toward personal growth based on your empowerment plan. Review your intentions regularly and adapt your plan as necessary to stay aligned with your core values and the principles of EHT.

8 Strategies to Decrease Distractions

Mindful Breathing: Practice deep and mindful breathing regularly throughout the day. Take a few moments to focus solely on your breath, observing each inhale and exhale. This practice can ground you in the present moment and help you refocus your attention when distractions arise.

Create a Distraction Journal: Keep a journal to record the times when you find yourself most distracted. Identify common patterns or triggers that lead to distractions. By becoming aware of these patterns, you can take proactive steps to minimize or avoid them.

Set Clear Intentions: Start each day by setting clear intentions for what you want to accomplish. Knowing your priorities will help you stay focused and make it easier to recognize and avoid distractions that may lead you off track.

Time Blocking: Divide your work or study time into blocks and assign specific tasks to each block. By creating a structured schedule, you are less likely to be swayed by distractions because you know what you should be doing at any given moment.

Mindful Technology Use: Be conscious of how you use technology, particularly social media and other apps that can easily lead to time-wasting distractions. Set limits on screen time and designate specific periods for checking emails and messages.

Check Your Environment: Be aware of your physical surroundings and how they might contribute to distractions. Minimize noise, clutter, and other potential disruptions that can take your focus away from the task at hand.

Practice Single-Tasking: Train yourself to focus on one task at a time rather than multitasking. Multitasking can reduce overall productivity and lead to more distractions. Stay present and give your full attention to each task before moving on to the next.

Regular Self-Reflection: Take time to reflect on your daily experiences and assess how well you manage distractions. Celebrate moments of success and identify areas where you can improve your focus. Regular self-reflection can help you fine-tune your self-awareness and sharpen your ability to limit distractions.

5 Exercises to Practice Acceptance and Non-Attachment

Leaves on a Stream:
Find a peaceful spot near a flowing stream or river or imagine one in your mind.

As thoughts or emotions arise, visualize them as leaves floating on the stream.

Watch them gently float by without grasping onto them or getting carried away.

Practice being an observer of your thoughts and emotions without judgment or attachment.

Cloud Watching:

Lie down on the grass or sit in a comfortable position outdoors, where you have a clear view of the sky.

As thoughts and emotions arise, visualize them as clouds passing by in the sky.

Observe each cloud without getting entangled in its form or story.

Let the clouds drift away, acknowledging that they come and go naturally.

Writing and Burning:

Grab a journal and write down any thoughts, emotions, or attachments that you feel are causing you stress or holding you back. Read each entry with awareness and acceptance of what you're feeling.

Afterward, take the pages outside and safely burn them, symbolizing the release of those thoughts and emotions. *Consider publishing your story and sharing it with others as an alternative to burning it.*

Bubble Bursting:

Imagine your thoughts and emotions as bubbles floating around you.

Observe each bubble as it appears, acknowledging its presence.

Then, visualize gently bursting each bubble with your breath, allowing the thoughts and emotions to dissipate.

Tossing Pebbles:

Find a quiet space near a body of water or an open field.

Pick up a small pebble and assign it a specific thought or emotion.

Stand at the water's edge or in the open field, and with each throw of the pebble, let go of that thought or emotion, allowing it to be released.

A Simple Breathing Exercise That Focuses on Extending Exhalations

Find a comfortable seated position with your back straight and your feet planted firmly on the ground.

Close your eyes and take a few deep breaths, inhaling slowly through your nose and exhaling through your mouth.

On your next inhale, count to four as you fill your lungs with air.

Hold your breath for a moment, and then exhale slowly through your mouth, counting to six as you release the air from your lungs.

Once you have fully exhaled, hold your breath for a moment before repeating the cycle of inhaling, holding, and exhaling for a few more rounds.

As you continue this exercise, try to focus on extending your exhalations even more, counting to seven or eight or even longer, if possible.

Remember to breathe slowly and steadily and avoid straining or forcing your breath. If you feel lightheaded or uncomfortable at any point, take a break and return to normal breathing. With practice, this exercise can help you calm your mind, reduce stress, and improve your overall breathing habits.

Sensory Awareness Exercise

Find a comfortable position, either sitting in an upright and dignified position or lying down flat on your back. Take a moment to settle into your body, allowing yourself to relax and let go of any tension.

Soften the muscles in your face, relax the muscles in your shoulders and feel your body relax from head to toe while following the full sensation of each breath and it enters and leaves your body.

Notice the sensation of the air entering and leaving your body. Pay attention to the rise and fall of your chest or the feeling of your abdomen expanding and contracting with each breath.

Now shift your attention to your body.
Slowly scan your body from head to toe, paying attention to any sensations or areas of tension you notice. Be curious and non-judgmental about what you observe.

Move your focus to your sense of touch.
Pay attention to the sensation of your body contacting any surface, such as the chair or floor beneath you. Notice the feeling of the object against your skin, the temperature of the air on your body, or any other tactile sensations you become aware of.

When you are ready, gradually shift your attention to your sense of hearing. Tune in to the sounds around you, both near and far. Notice any background noises, the hum of appliances or the sounds of nature.

Also, pay attention to any sounds within your own body, like your heartbeat or your breath.

Next, bring your awareness to your sense of smell. Take a deep breath in and notice any scents or smells in the environment. Maybe it's the aroma of food, the scent of flowers, or any other odors that come to your attention.

Finally, direct your attention to your sense of sight. Observe the objects and colors in your immediate surroundings without focusing on anything. Observe without judgment. Name the shapes, colors textures and objects you notice.

As you close this practice, take a moment to reflect on your experience. Notice any changes in your awareness or any insights that may have arisen during the exercise.

Ideal Self Visualization

Find a comfortable position, either sitting in an upright and dignified position or lying down flat on your back. Take a moment to settle into your body, allowing yourself to relax and let go of any tension.

Soften the muscles in your face. relax the muscles in your shoulders and feel your body relax from head to toe while following the full sensation of each breath and it enters and leaves your body.

Once you feel relaxed, start visualizing an ideal version of yourself. Imagine yourself as the best possible version of who you are.

Visualize all of your most positive qualities, traits, and behaviors and all that you aspire to possess.
Engage all your senses in this visualization.

See yourself in your mind's eye, radiating with confidence and positivity. Hear the positive thoughts and empowering words that your best self would use.

Feel the emotions of happiness, fulfillment, and contentment that comes with being your best self.

As you continue the visualization, focus on specific areas of your life where you want to see improvement. It could be in relationships, career, personal growth, health, or any other area that matters to you.

Visualize yourself excelling in those areas, achieving your goals, and experiencing success and satisfaction.

Stay in this visualization for as long as you'd like to immerse yourself in the positive feelings and energy. Allow yourself to fully embrace these qualities so that you can better cultivate them outside of this visualization of your best self. When you'd like, slowly bring your awareness back to the present moment.

Take a few moments to reflect on the experience. Consider the qualities and behaviors you visualized and how you can integrate them into your daily life. Set small, actionable goals that can help you embody your best self.

Remember, this exercise is meant to create awareness and inspire positive change. Regular practice can help you align your thoughts, beliefs, and actions with your best self, leading to personal growth and fulfillment.

Visualization To Enhance Self Awareness

Find a comfortable position, either sitting in an upright and dignified position or lying down flat on your back.

Take a moment to settle into your body, allowing yourself to relax and let go of any tension.

Soften the muscles in your face, relax the muscles in your shoulders and feel your body relax from head to toe. Notice your breath, don't try to change it in any way, simply notice it.

As you inhale, imagine breathing in calmness, and as you exhale, imagine letting go of any tension or stress you may be carrying. Continue breathing and noticing for about 30 seconds to a minute.

To begin enhancing self-awareness, recall a situation or experience that you would like to explore with greater self-awareness. It could be a pattern of behavior that you've noticed in yourself, a relationship dynamic that you want to understand better, or a challenge that you're facing in your life.

As you consider and choose this area, continue to follow the sensation of each breath. Once you've selected the situation or experience, you'd like to gain further insight into, continue to the next steps.

Take a moment to observe your thoughts and feelings in relation to this situation or experience. Observe them without judgment.

Now, imagine that you are stepping back from this situation or experience, and view it from a more objective perspective.

What do you notice?

What patterns or themes emerge?

What new insights or perspectives can you uncover?

As you explore, engage with a sense of deep curiosity. As if you were an inquisitive child.

To conclude this practice, take notes and record your new insights. As you move forward use these new insights in ways that empower yourself and honor the dignity of the community around you.

Visualization For Managing Emotions

Find a comfortable position, either sitting in an upright and dignified position or lying down flat on your back.

Begin settling into your body. Take a moment to relax and let go of any tension. Soften the muscles in your face, relax the muscles in your shoulders and feel your body relax from head to toe while following the full sensation of each breath and it enters and leaves your body.

Imagine yourself standing beside a lake. This lake represents your emotional state. Usually it's calm, even serene, sometimes there are ripples and sometimes there are waves. Take a moment to stand on the bank and observe the lake's current state. Simply observe it as an outsider, without judgment and with compassion.

Take a moment to observe the surface of the lake. Notice how areas are calm and still. As you look closer, you may see some ripples on the lake's surface. Observe them without judgment, noticing the colors, textures, and movements.

As you continue to observe the ripples, take a deep breath and imagine a gentle breeze blowing across the surface of the lake. This breeze represents your breath and its ability to help you manage your emotions.

As you breathe in, imagine yourself drawing in a calm, peaceful energy. As you breathe out, imagine yourself releasing any tension, anxiety, or negative emotions.

Keep breathing deeply and slowly, allowing the gentle breeze to guide the ripples on the surface of the lake. Notice the ripples slowly fade away, and with each breath, feel a sense of calm and relaxation washing over you and the ripples fade more.

If a new ripple appears simply observe it and use your breath to guide it to calm. Allow yourself to experience it without judgment, and let it pass with each breath. When you're ready, imagine yourself walking away from the lake and back into the present moment.

As you bring your awareness back to your body, take a few deep breaths to ground yourself and feel the sense of peace and relaxation that you gained from this visualization.

Recall this practice when you notice the ripples and waves of Lake Life popping up so that you can manage the moment in empowering and dignified ways.

Visualization Exercise to Reduce Stress and Tension

Find a quiet and comfortable space where you can sit or lie down without distractions.

Go ahead and find a comfortable position, either sitting in an upright and dignified position or lying down flat on your back.

Take a moment to settle into your body, allowing yourself to relax and let go of any tension. Soften the muscles in your face, relax the muscles in your shoulders and feel your body relax from head to toe.

Take a moment to notice the natural rhythm of your breathing. Now feel the sensation of the breath entering and leaving your body. Allow your breath to become slow, deep, and steady.

Once you feel grounded in your breath, imagine yourself in a peaceful and serene location. It could be a place you have been to before or a completely imaginary place. It might be a beach, a forest, a garden, or any other setting that brings you a sense of calm and tranquility.

As you visualize this place, engage your senses. Imagine the sights around you — the colors, the textures, and the beauty of the surroundings.

Visualize the gentle movement of leaves, the sparkling of sunlight, or the ebb and flow of ocean waves.

Now, focus on the sounds of this peaceful place. Imagine the soothing sounds that you would hear- the rustling of leaves, the gentle lapping of water, the chirping of birds, or any other sounds that bring you comfort and relaxation.

Now, turn your attention to the sensations in your body. Visualize yourself sitting or lying down in this serene location. Feel the warmth of the sun on your skin or the coolness of a gentle breeze.

Sense the softness of the sand, the grass, or any other surfaces you may be in contact with.

Take a moment to notice any scents in the air.

Visualize the aroma of flowers, the freshness of the sea breeze, or any other fragrances that you associate with this peaceful place.

Allow yourself to fully immerse in these sensory experiences. As you continue to visualize this serene location, let go of any tension or stress that you may be holding in your body. With each breath, imagine releasing any physical or mental tension.

Visualize the stress melting away and being carried away by the gentle breeze or absorbed by the earth beneath you. You can choose to stay in the same location or explore different aspects of the peaceful setting.

Trust your imagination and let it guide you toward a state of deep relaxation.

Stay in this visualization for as long as you like.

When you are ready to conclude the exercise, take a few deep breaths and gradually bring your awareness back to the present moment.

Remember, the purpose of this exercise is to use the power of your imagination and visualization to reduce stress and tension. Practice regularly to strengthen your ability to evoke a sense of calm and relaxation whenever you need it.

Visualization To Increase Motivation

Find a comfortable position, either sitting in an upright and dignified position or lying down flat on your back. Take a moment to settle into your body, allowing yourself to relax and let go of any tension.

Soften the muscles in your face, relax the muscles in your shoulders and feel your body relax from head to toe. Take a moment to notice the natural rhythm of your breathing.

Imagine yourself standing at the bottom of a tall, majestic mountain. The mountain represents your goals and aspirations, and you are going to climb it with focus and determination. Look up at the mountain and see the peak in the distance.

Notice the slope, the texture of the rocks, and the vegetation around you. Take in the sights and sounds of the environment. As you start to climb the mountain, focus on each step you take. Feel the strength and stability in your legs, the power in your core, and the rhythm of your breath.

With each step, you feel more and more motivated to reach the top. You are filled with a sense of purpose and determination.

As you climb higher, you encounter some obstacles, Some loose rocks and slippery terrain. Instead of getting discouraged, you approach these challenges with a calm and focused mind.

You find ways to overcome them, either by finding a different path or by using your skills and strength to push through. There's a work around for everything.

As you approach the summit, you can see a breathtaking view from the top. You feel a sense of accomplishment and pride for making it this far. Take it all in and reflect on your journey to the summit.

Take a moment and rest to appreciate the view.

Feel the sun on your face, the wind in your hair, and the sense of achievement in your heart. When you are ready, take a deep breath and start your descent back down.

Remember that the journey down can be just as rewarding as the climb up. Take each step with a sense of ease and gratitude. As you reach the bottom of the mountain, bring your awareness back to your body. Take a few deep breaths to ground yourself and feel the renewed sense of motivation and purpose that you gained from this visualization.

Visualization For Creativity Enhancement

Find a comfortable position, either sitting in an upright and dignified position or lying down flat on your back. Take a moment to settle into your body, allowing yourself to relax and let go of any tension.

Soften the muscles in your face, relax the muscles in your shoulders and feel your body relax from head to toe. Take a moment to notice the natural rhythm of your breathing.

Now Imagine yourself standing in a spacious, well-lit room that is completely empty. This room represents the blank canvas of your mind, and you are going to fill it with creativity and imagination.

Take a moment to observe the space and the light pouring in from the windows. Allow yourself to feel open and receptive to new ideas and inspiration.

As you stand in the empty room, visualize a door appearing in front of you. This door represents your imagination and the infinite possibilities that lie beyond it.

Take a deep breath and open the door.

As you step through the threshold, allow your imagination to run wild. Imagine colors, shapes, and textures swirling around you in a beautiful and chaotic dance.

As you explore this new world, allow yourself to be completely present and curious. Observe the colors, textures, and shapes that you encounter without any preconceived notions or expectations.

Allow yourself to become completely absorbed in this world of creativity and imagination.

Take your time and enjoy the process of exploring new ideas and possibilities.

As you stand in the empty room once again, take a moment to reflect on the beauty and creativity that you encountered.

Stay here as long as you'd like and return to this place anytime you wish.

When you're ready to come back to the present moment and conclude this practice, take a deep breath and imagine yourself stepping back through the door and into the empty room.

Take this sense of creativity and imagination with you as you go about your day and remember to allow yourself to explore new ideas and possibilities with an open and non-judgmental mind.

A Meditation on Boundary-Setting

Find a comfortable position, either sitting in an upright and dignified position or lying down flat on your back.

Take a moment to settle into your body, allowing yourself to relax and let go of any tension.

Soften the muscles in your face, relax the muscles in your shoulders and feel your body relax from head to toe.

Take a moment to notice the natural rhythm of your breathing.

Bring to mind a situation or relationship where you feel that your boundaries have been crossed or are not being honored.

Begin to visualize yourself as a strong and confident person, capable of setting clear and healthy boundaries.

Now Imagine a bright and powerful light surrounding you, protecting you from any harm or negativity.

Take a deep breath and visualize a line or barrier that you can use to set your boundaries.

This line can be physical, like a fence or a wall, or it can be a symbol that represents your inner strength and self-respect.

Imagine yourself setting this boundary with kindness and assertiveness. Say to yourself,

 "I deserve to be treated with dignity and kindness, and I am confident in my ability to set healthy boundaries."

As you set your boundary, visualize any negative or harmful energy bouncing off of the line or barrier and dissipating into the atmosphere.

Take a few deep breaths and feel the strength and power of your boundary. Notice how it feels to be protected and honored.

When you're ready to conclude this practice, take a deep breath and visualize yourself stepping away from the boundary and into the present moment.

Cary a sense of strength and confidence with you as you go about your day.

Appendix B
Practices That Celebrate Our Common Humanity

The following section contains multiple practices that celebrate our common humanity. Engaging in these practices helps develop the EHT attitude, Cultivating A Dignity Lens. Explore all practices and return to the ones you find meaningful. This is not a comprehensive list as the number of possible practices is infinite. As you familiarize yourself with the practices named here, think about other possible practices that celebrate our common humanity you can authentically engage in.

Thinking about the positive impact these practices have regarding brain health and well-being combined with the neuroplasticity principle of "we become what we practice," consider adding the practices you find meaningful into your habits and routines to create an empowering and dignified life.

Writing Exercise to Honor the Dignity of Your Whole Self

Set aside some quiet and uninterrupted time for yourself. Find a comfortable space where you can reflect and write without distractions.

Take a few deep breaths to ground yourself in the present moment. Close your eyes and allow your mind to settle.

Begin by contemplating the concept of dignity. Reflect on what it means to you and how it manifests in your life. Consider the importance of honoring and valuing your whole self—your strengths, weaknesses, successes, failures, and everything in between.

Open your eyes and pick up a pen and paper or open a blank document on your computer. Write the heading: "Honoring the Dignity of My Whole Self."

Start by expressing gratitude for your body. Write down three things you appreciate about your physical self. Focus on aspects such as strength, resilience, beauty, or any other qualities that come to mind.

Move on to acknowledging your emotions and feelings. Write about a recent experience where you handled your emotions with grace or showed resilience in the face of challenges.

Reflect on how your emotions contribute to your unique human experience.

Next, explore your accomplishments and talents. Write down three achievements or skills that you are proud of. Consider the hard work, dedication, and personal growth that went into each one.

Reflect on your vulnerabilities and areas where you may struggle. Write about a particular challenge you are facing or a personal trait that you often perceive as a weakness. Embrace these aspects of yourself with compassion and understanding.

Consider your values and beliefs. Write about the principles and convictions that guide your actions and decisions. Reflect on how these values contribute to your sense of self and the impact they have on the world around you.

Take a moment to write a message of self-acceptance and self-compassion. Offer kind words to yourself, acknowledging that you are deserving of love, and dignity in all aspects of your being.

Read through what you have written, allowing the words to resonate within you. Reflect on the wholeness and complexity of your identity, appreciating the unique tapestry that makes you who you are.

Consider any insights or lessons that have emerged from this writing exercise. Reflect on how you can continue honoring the dignity of your whole self in your daily life.

Writing Exercise That Emphasizes Our Common Humanity Rather Than Assigned Identity Groups

Take a pen and paper or open a blank document on your computer. Start by writing down the heading: "Our Shared Humanity."

Reflect on the qualities and experiences that are universally human. Think about the emotions, desires, and needs that every person, regardless of their identity groups, shares. Consider the following prompts and write freely without judgment:

What are some fundamental emotions that all humans experience?

What are some universal desires or aspirations that cut across cultural or societal boundaries?

What are some basic needs that every person requires to live a fulfilling life?

What are some experiences or life events that connect us as human beings?

Use the prompts as inspiration to write a paragraph or a few sentences for each reflection. Dive deep into the essence of our shared humanity. Focus on commonalities rather than differences.

Challenge yourself to think beyond stereotypes or preconceived notions associated with identity groups.

Instead, explore the shared experiences and values that transcend those categories.
Feel free to incorporate personal anecdotes, examples, or observations to illustrate your points. This can add depth and authenticity to your writing.

As you write, remind yourself of the interconnectedness of human experiences. Emphasize the understanding that we all have our unique stories, yet there are threads that bind us together.

Take your time to reflect, revise, and refine your writing. Craft your sentences with care to express the depth of our shared humanity.

Once you feel satisfied with your piece, take a moment to read it aloud or silently to yourself. Absorb the words and let their meaning resonate within you.

Consider sharing your writing with others or keeping it as a personal reminder of our shared humanity. By sharing your reflections, you can inspire conversations and promote understanding among those who encounter your words.

8 Strategies to Honor the Dignity of a Close Friend

Reflect on their positive qualities: Take a few moments to think about your friend and all the positive qualities that you admire in them. Consider their kindness, intelligence, humor, compassion, or any other traits that make them special. Write down these qualities on a piece of paper or in a journal.

Write a gratitude letter: Take some time to compose a heartfelt gratitude letter to your friend. Express your appreciation for their presence in your life and how they have positively impacted you. Be specific about the qualities and actions you admire and the ways they have enriched your friendship. Let them know how much their dignity and worth mean to you.

Plan a meaningful activity: Think about an activity or gesture that would honor your friend's dignity and make them feel valued. It could be something as simple as cooking their favorite meal, planning a surprise outing, or organizing a gathering of friends to celebrate them. Consider their preferences and interests and choose something that would resonate with them personally.

Spend quality time together: Schedule a time to spend quality time with your friend. During this time, be fully present and engaged. Listen attentively, engage in meaningful conversations, and genuinely connect with them. Show them that their thoughts, feelings, and experiences matter to you.

Practice active appreciation: Throughout your interactions, consciously look for opportunities to appreciate and acknowledge your friend's dignity. Offer sincere compliments, affirm their strengths, and show genuine interest in their perspectives and dreams. Make them feel seen, heard, and valued.

Support their goals and aspirations: Encourage and support your friend in pursuing their goals and dreams. Help, guidance, or resources whenever you can. Help them recognize their own worth and potential by believing in their abilities and providing a safe space for them to explore their passions.

Practice dignity and compassion: Seek to understand their experiences and challenges without judgment. Be a source of comfort, support, and understanding during difficult times.

Reflect on your friendship: Take time to reflect on your friendship. Appreciate the journey you've shared, the growth you've experienced together, and the lessons you've learned. Recognize the reciprocal nature of your relationship and the ways in which both of you contribute to each other's dignity.

Remember, the key is to approach this exercise with sincerity, authenticity, and love. By actively honoring the dignity of your close friend, you can strengthen your bond and create a meaningful and uplifting experience for both of you.

Exercise To Honor the Dignity of Strangers

Honoring the dignity of strangers is an important practice for cultivating compassion and understanding towards others, even when we don't know them personally. Here's an exercise that can help you to honor the dignity of strangers:

Start by acknowledging that every person has inherent worth and dignity, regardless of their background or circumstances.

Recognize that each person you encounter, even strangers, has their own unique experiences, feelings, and perspectives.

Practice being present and attentive when interacting with strangers. This means putting away distractions, like your phone or other devices, and focusing your attention on the person in front of you.

Practice active listening when speaking with strangers. Ask questions to learn more about their experiences and perspectives and try to understand their point of view as fully as possible.

Look for opportunities to show kindness and compassion to strangers, even in small ways. This could be as simple as offering a smile or a friendly greeting or helping someone with a task or carrying something heavy.

Cultivate a sense of compassion towards strangers. Try to imagine their experience from their perspective and cultivate a sense of kindness and understanding towards them.

Finally, remember that small acts of kindness and compassion towards strangers can have a big impact.

By honoring the dignity of strangers, we can build stronger, more compassionate communities where everyone feels valued.

Remember, honoring the dignity of strangers is a practice that takes time and effort. By approaching interactions with strangers with an open mind and a compassionate heart, we can build a more connected and dignified world.

Exercise Honoring the Dignity of Someone You Disagree With

Choose a specific person with whom you hold a disagreement or a different perspective. It could be a friend, family member, colleague, or even a public figure. The key is to select someone with whom you genuinely differ on a particular issue.

Find a quiet and comfortable space where you can reflect without distractions. Take a few deep breaths to center yourself and cultivate a calm and open mindset. Begin by acknowledging the inherent worth and dignity of every individual, regardless of their opinions or beliefs. Remind yourself that each person is entitled to their own thoughts and perspectives, and their dignity should be honored.

Reflect on the reasons why you disagree with this person. Consider their arguments, viewpoints, or actions that have led to your differing opinions. Take a moment to understand your own emotions and reactions toward their stance.

Now, shift your focus to understanding the person as a whole. Think about their background, life experiences, values, and beliefs that might have shaped their perspective. Try to put yourself in their shoes and empathize with their unique journey.

Write down three positive qualities or strengths that you recognize in this person, unrelated to your disagreement. Consider their contributions, skills, or any admirable aspects you can identify.

This exercise helps to humanize them beyond the issue you disagree on.

Reflect on the values you hold dear and consider how those values may also be important to the person you disagree with. Look for common ground or shared concerns that could be the basis for a deeper understanding.

Write a compassionate letter to this person, expressing your desire to honor their dignity despite your differences. Share your perspective calmly and clearly, focusing on understanding rather than persuading or proving them wrong. Avoid personal attacks or derogatory language.

Read the letter aloud or silently to yourself, imagining a compassionate and open-hearted dialogue between you and the person. Visualize a dignified exchange of ideas and a genuine effort to find common ground.

Take a moment to reflect on the emotions that arose during the exercise. Observe any shifts in your perspective or newfound compassion towards the person you disagree with.

Consider how you can apply the principles of dignity, understanding, and compassion in your interactions with this person going forward. Reflect on the possibilities for constructive dialogue or finding areas of agreement without compromising your own values.
Remember, this exercise is not about changing your beliefs or conceding your own values. It is about recognizing the inherent dignity of the person you disagree with and fostering a compassionate approach to understanding their perspective.

Exercise to Maintain Dignity
During Conflict with Another Person

Start by taking a few deep breaths to help you relax and center yourself. Allow your body to release any tension or stress you may be feeling.

As you prepare to engage in conflict with the other person, remind yourself that you are worthy of respect and dignity.

Affirm to yourself that you have the right to express your thoughts and feelings, and to be treated with kindness and consideration.

When engaging in conflict, try to remain calm and grounded. Take a moment to pause and reflect before responding, rather than reacting impulsively.

This can help you to respond from a place of centeredness and thoughtfulness, rather than defensiveness or anger.

Focus on using "I" statements, rather than "you" statements. For example, instead of saying, "You always do this," say "I feel hurt when this happens."

This can help the other person to see your perspective without feeling attacked or criticized.

Be willing to listen to the other person's point of view. Try to understand their perspective, even if you don't agree with it. This can help to de-escalate the conflict and promote mutual understanding.

Finally, remind yourself that conflicts can be resolved without compromising your dignity. Even if the other person does not agree with you or apologize, you can still maintain your sense of worth and dignity by standing up for yourself and expressing your needs in a dignified way.

Remember, conflict is a natural part of any relationship, and it is an opportunity to grow and learn from each other. By maintaining your dignity during conflicts, you can build stronger, more compassionate relationships with others.

Communication Exercise to Honor Dignity Without Attacking or Blaming Others

Start by identifying a specific need or feeling that you would like to express. Be as clear and specific as possible.

Begin your communication by sharing how you are feeling, using "I" statements. For example, "I feel frustrated," or "I feel overwhelmed."

Next, identify the need or value that is underlying your feeling. For example, if you are feeling frustrated, the underlying need might be for more support or understanding.

Avoid blaming or attacking others for your feelings. Instead, focus on expressing your own needs and emotions in a way that invites understanding and connection.

Use non-judgmental language to describe the situation and avoid making assumptions about the other person's intentions or motivations. Stick to the facts and describe your own experience as objectively as possible.

Finally, be open to the other person's perspective, and be willing to engage in a dialogue to find a mutually acceptable solution. Practice active listening and strive to understand the other person's needs and feelings as well.

Exercise To Find
Common Ground and Compromise

Identify the issue: Start by identifying the issue that needs to be addressed. Write down a brief description of the issue in a neutral and objective manner.

Identify the stakeholders: Next, identify the stakeholders involved in the issue. Write down the names of all the people or groups who are affected by the issue.

Identify the interests: For each stakeholder, identify their interests in the issue. What do they want or need? Write down a list of interests for each stakeholder.

Identify areas of agreement: Look for areas of agreement or overlap between the interests of the stakeholders. Write down these areas of agreement.

Identify areas of disagreement: Next, identify the areas of disagreement or conflict between the interests of the stakeholders. Write down these areas of disagreement.

Brainstorm solutions: With the areas of agreement and disagreement in mind, brainstorm potential solutions to the issue. Encourage all stakeholders to contribute ideas and work together to find solutions that meet the needs of everyone involved. Write down all potential solutions.

Evaluate and select a solution: Evaluate each potential solution based on its ability to meet the interests of all stakeholders.

Select the solution that best meets the needs of everyone involved.

Implement and monitor the solution: Once a solution has been selected, implement it and monitor its effectiveness. Adjust as necessary to ensure that the solution continues to meet the needs of all stakeholders.

By following these steps, you can find common ground and compromise with others involved in an issue and develop a solution that meets the needs of everyone involved. This exercise can help improve relationships, build trust, and create more positive outcomes.

Exercise To Honor Self-Dignity During Difficult and Challenging Times

Honoring your own dignity during difficult and challenging times is an important practice for cultivating self-dignity and resilience. Here's an exercise that can help you to honor your own dignity during these times:

Start by taking a few deep breaths to help you relax and center yourself. Allow your body to release any tension or stress you may be feeling.

Acknowledge that you have inherent worth and dignity, regardless of the challenges you are facing. Remind yourself that you have the right to express your thoughts and feelings, and to be treated with kindness and consideration.

Practice self-compassion. This means treating yourself with the same kindness and understanding that you would offer to a close friend or family member. Be gentle with yourself and acknowledge the difficult feelings you may be experiencing.

Look for ways to take care of yourself during difficult times. This could be as simple as taking a few minutes to practice mindfulness or meditation or doing something that brings you joy and comfort.

Surround yourself with supportive people. Reach out to friends or family members who can offer a listening ear or seek out professional support if needed.

Finally, remind yourself that difficult times are a natural part of life, and that you have the strength and resilience to get through them. Honor your own resilience and strength, and trust in your ability to overcome challenges.

Remember, honoring your own dignity during difficult times is a practice that takes time and effort. By treating yourself with kindness, compassion, and dignity you can cultivate a stronger sense of resilience and well-being.

Exercise To Explore and Express Vulnerability

Find a quiet and comfortable space where you feel safe and at ease. You may want to have a journal or a blank piece of paper and a pen nearby.

Take a few moments to reflect on your own emotions and experiences. Consider areas of your life where you feel vulnerable or have difficulty expressing vulnerability.

It could be related to personal relationships, fears, past experiences, or self-doubts.

Choose one aspect of vulnerability that you would like to explore and express. It could be a specific emotion, an experience, or a current struggle. Identify what you feel comfortable sharing at this moment.

Write a letter or journal entry addressed to yourself or someone you trust deeply. Begin by acknowledging your vulnerability and the specific aspect you have chosen to explore. You can start with phrases like:

"I want to share something that makes me feel vulnerable..."
"I've been reflecting on an experience that has left me feeling vulnerable..."
"In this moment, I feel the need to express my vulnerability about..."

Describe the feelings, thoughts, and experiences associated with your chosen aspect of vulnerability. Be honest and authentic in your expression.

Allow yourself to fully delve into your emotions and provide context for your vulnerability.

Consider why this aspect of vulnerability is important to you. Reflect on the impact it has on your life, relationships, or personal growth. Explore any lessons or insights you have gained from navigating this vulnerability.

If you feel comfortable, you can choose to share this letter or journal entry with someone you trust. Sharing your vulnerability with others can deepen connections and create space for support and understanding.

However, it is completely okay to keep it for your personal reflection if that feels more appropriate for you at this time.

After writing, take a moment to reflect on the process and the emotions that surfaced during the exercise.

Allow yourself to feel any emotions that may have arisen and offer yourself self-compassion and kindness.

Remember, expressing vulnerability is a personal and individual process. Take your time, honor your own boundaries, and only share as much as feels right for you.

An Exercise to Increase and Build Trust

Find a partner or group of people with whom you want to build trust. This exercise is most effective when done with someone you feel comfortable and safe with.

Sit down together in a quiet and comfortable space where you can have an uninterrupted conversation.

Start by discussing the concept of trust. Share your own understanding of trust and what it means to you. Talk about why trust is important in relationships and the benefits it brings.

Reflect on any past experiences that may have impacted your trust in others. Share your feelings, thoughts, and lessons learned from those experiences. This sharing should be done with vulnerability and openness.

Take turns asking each other questions related to trust. These questions can be personal and meaningful, aimed at understanding each other on a deeper level. Some examples include:

"What actions or behaviors help you trust someone?"
"What are some experiences that have made it difficult for you to trust?"
"What can I do to earn your trust?"
"What are your expectations regarding trust in this relationship?"

As the questions are asked, practice active listening. Give your full attention to the person speaking, showing compassion, and understanding.
Avoid judgment or interruption.

After each person has answered a question, take a moment to reflect on their response. Share your thoughts, feelings, or any insights that arose from their answer.

Use this opportunity to deepen your understanding of each other.

Engage in trust-building activities. These activities can vary depending on the nature of your relationship and your comfort level.

They may include sharing personal stories, engaging in collaborative tasks, or participating in team-building exercises.

The goal is to create experiences that foster trust, cooperation, and open communication.

Throughout the exercise, be patient and compassionate with one another. Building trust takes time, and it is essential to each person's boundaries and comfort levels. Remember, trust is built through consistent actions and genuine interactions.
After completing the exercise, take a few moments to reflect on the conversation and activities. Consider what you have learned about trust and how you can apply those insights to your relationship moving forward.

Exercise to Restore Your Dignity
When It's Been Violated

Find a quiet and comfortable space where you can have
privacy and feel safe. Take a few moments to ground
yourself by focusing on your breath and allowing your
body to relax.

Acknowledge and validate your emotions. Give yourself
permission to feel whatever emotions arise because of the
dignity violation. It could be anger, sadness, frustration, or
a combination of various feelings.

 Recognize that these emotions are a natural response to
the situation. Remind yourself that you have inherent
worth and dignity that cannot be diminished by the
actions of others.

Affirm your self-worth and the qualities that make you
unique and valuable as a human being.

Reflect on the values that are important to you and the
standards by which you choose to live your life. Consider
how the dignity violation aligns or conflicts with these
values. Clarify your own principles and beliefs to ground
yourself in a sense of personal integrity.

Write a letter to yourself, addressing the dignity violation
directly. Describe the incident, expressing how it made
you feel and the impact it had on your sense of self-worth.

Validate your emotions and acknowledge the pain caused by the violation. Challenge any negative beliefs that may have arisen from the dignity violation. Write down positive affirmations that counteract those beliefs.

For example, if you feel unworthy or powerless, affirm statements such as "I am deserving of dignity" or "I have the strength to overcome this challenge."

Engage in self-care activities that nurture and restore your well-being. This could include engaging in hobbies you enjoy, spending time in nature, seeking support from loved ones, practicing mindfulness or meditation, or engaging in physical exercise.

Take care of your physical, mental, and emotional needs as you heal.

Practice forgiveness, not necessarily for the person who violated your dignity, but for yourself. Holding onto resentment and anger can hinder your own healing process.

Recognize that forgiveness is a personal choice and does not mean condoning the actions of others. It means freeing yourself from the emotional burden and allowing yourself to move forward.

Engage in activities that reaffirm your sense of dignity and self-worth. This could involve pursuing personal goals, engaging in acts of self-expression, volunteering for a cause you believe in, or surrounding yourself with positive and supportive people.

Reflect on the lessons you have learned from the dignity violation. Identify any personal growth or insights that have emerged from the experience. Consider how you can use this experience to empower yourself and advocate for your own dignity in the future.

Remember, restoring your dignity is a personal journey that takes time and self-compassion. Be patient with yourself as you heal and seek professional support if needed.

Surround yourself with people who uplift and validate your dignity and continue to engage in practices that nurture your self-worth. You have the power to reclaim and restore your dignity, even in the face of adversity.

Exercise To Restore the Dignity of Another Person When You Violated Their Dignity

Acknowledge and reflect on your actions. Take time to honestly assess the ways in which you violated the other person's dignity. Recognize the impact it had on them and the importance of taking responsibility for your behavior.

Approach the person with humility and sincerity. Express your genuine remorse for the harm you caused and your commitment to making amends. Choose an appropriate setting and time to have a private conversation.

Begin the conversation by apologizing sincerely and without making excuses. Use "I" statements to take full responsibility for your actions. For example, say,

"I am truly sorry for what I said/did. It violated your dignity, and I deeply regret it."

Give the person an opportunity to express their feelings and emotions. Listen attentively and without interruption, allowing them to share their experiences and the impact your actions had on them.

Ask the person if there is anything specific, they need or expect from you to restore their dignity. Be open and receptive to their requests, acknowledging that you may not be able to fully undo the harm but are committed to making sincere efforts to repair the damage.

Reflect on what you have learned from this experience and how you can grow from it. Consider the underlying beliefs or biases that contributed to your actions and commit to unlearning them. Engage in personal growth activities, such as reading, attending workshops, or seeking therapy, to gain a deeper understanding of dignity, compassion, and connectedness.

Take action to rectify the situation and restore the person's dignity. This may involve specific actions or gestures requested by the person. Follow through on your commitments and demonstrate genuine change in your behavior and attitudes.

Cultivate a culture of dignity in your interactions with others moving forward. Treat everyone with kindness and consideration. Actively challenge any biases or prejudices you may hold and strive to create a more empowering and dignified environment.

Periodically check in with the person to ensure they feel heard and valued. Offer ongoing support and make yourself available for further conversations if they wish to express their feelings or address any concerns.
Be patient and understanding throughout the process.

Restoring someone's dignity takes time, and healing is a personal journey for both parties involved. Allow the person to set the pace for reconciliation and offer them the space they need to process their emotions.

8 Strategies to Maintain Dignity During Disagreement

Stay calm and composed: Keep your emotions in check and avoid reacting impulsively. Take deep breaths, center yourself, and approach disagreement with a calm and composed demeanor. This will help you maintain control over your words and actions.

Listen actively: Practice active listening by giving your full attention to the other person's perspective. Avoid interrupting or dismissing their point of view. Show dignity by genuinely seeking to understand their thoughts and feelings.

Choose your words carefully: Use dignified and considerate language when expressing your own thoughts and feelings. Avoid personal attacks, name-calling, or derogatory language. Focus on the issues at hand rather than attacking the person.

Express yourself assertively: Assertiveness allows you to communicate your needs, boundaries, and opinions while honoring the other person's perspective. Clearly and confidently articulate your thoughts, using "I" statements to express your feelings and opinions without blaming or accusing.

Seek common ground: Look for areas of agreement or shared values that can serve as a foundation for finding a resolution. Emphasize points of agreement to build rapport and demonstrate that you value the other person's perspective, even if you disagree on certain aspects.

Practice compassion and understanding: Put yourself in the other person's shoes and try to understand their underlying motivations, fears, or concerns. Be compassionate by acknowledging their feelings and seek to understand their experiences, even if you don't agree with their conclusions.

Maintain dignified body language: Non-verbal cues play a significant role in communication. Maintain open and non-threatening body language, such as making eye contact, using open gestures, and avoiding aggressive postures. Be mindful of your facial expressions and tone of voice, aiming for a dignified and composed demeanor.

Focus on problem-solving: Shift the focus from blame or winning arguments to finding a mutually beneficial solution. Collaborate with the other person to identify common goals and brainstorm possible solutions.

Restoring Dignity After Experiencing Harm and Indignity

Acknowledge and validate your feelings: Begin by recognizing and validating the emotions that arise from the harm and indignity you experienced. Allow yourself to feel anger, sadness, or any other emotions that come up. Understand that your feelings are valid and deserving of acknowledgment.

Practice self-compassion: Treat yourself with kindness and compassion during this challenging time. Remind yourself that experiencing harm and indignity does not diminish your worth as a person. Offer yourself gentle and supportive words of understanding, just as you would to a close friend going through a difficult situation.

Engage in self-reflection: Take time to reflect on the situation that caused harm or indignity. Consider your boundaries, values, and needs. Reflect on what happened and how it affected you. Ask yourself what you can learn from the experience and how you can grow stronger and wiser as a result.

Seek support: Reach out to trusted friends, family, or professionals who can provide support and guidance. Share your experience with those who will listen without judgment and offer compassion and understanding. Their support can help validate your feelings and provide a sense of belonging and connection.

Set boundaries: Clearly define your boundaries and communicate them assertively to others. Establishing healthy boundaries helps protect your dignity and ensures that your needs and values are honored. Practice saying "no" when necessary and prioritize self-care.

Engage in self-care activities: Engage in activities that nurture your well-being and promote self-compassion. This could include engaging in hobbies, practicing mindfulness or meditation, exercising, spending time in nature, journaling, or seeking professional support. Find activities that bring you joy, comfort, and a sense of renewal.

Foster self-empowerment: Take steps to regain your sense of agency and empowerment. Set small, achievable goals that align with your values and help rebuild your confidence. Celebrate your accomplishments along the way, no matter how small they may seem.

Practice forgiveness: Consider whether forgiveness is appropriate and healing for you in this situation. Forgiveness is a personal choice and may or may not be necessary for your healing process. If you choose to forgive, remember that it is about freeing yourself from the burden of resentment rather than condoning the harm done.

8 Strategies for Finding Commonalities with Another Person

Active listening: Engage in active listening by giving your full attention to the other person. Truly listen to their words, thoughts, and feelings without interrupting or jumping to conclusions. Show genuine interest in understanding their perspective.

Ask open-ended questions: Encourage meaningful conversation by asking open-ended questions that allow the other person to share more about themselves. Questions like "What are your passions?" or "What do you enjoy doing in your free time?" can help uncover shared interests and experiences.

Share personal stories: Open up about your own experiences, interests, and values. By sharing personal stories, you create an opportunity for the other person to relate and find common ground. Be authentic and vulnerable in your storytelling to foster a deeper connection.

Look for shared values and beliefs: Explore topics related to values and beliefs, such as family, spirituality, or personal growth. Discussing these areas can reveal shared values, moral principles, or philosophical outlooks, strengthening the sense of community.

Find common hobbies or interests: Discover shared hobbies or interests that you both enjoy. It could be sports, music, cooking, or any other activity. Engage in these shared activities together or discuss them to create a sense of camaraderie and shared enjoyment.

Seek common goals: Identify common goals or aspirations that you and the other person share. It could be personal, professional, or community-oriented goals. Working towards these shared objectives can foster a sense of collaboration, unity, and a feeling of being part of something bigger.

Practice perspective-taking: Seek to understand the other person's point of view, even if you initially disagree. Put yourself in their shoes and consider their background, experiences, and challenges. Look for commonalities in your human experiences and emotions.

Embrace diversity of people and thought to learn from differences: Appreciate and celebrate the differences between you and the other person. Recognize that diversity enriches our communities and provides opportunities for learning and growth.

A Meditation on Human Dignity

Find a comfortable position, either sitting in an upright and dignified position or lying down flat on your back. Take a moment to settle into your body, allowing yourself to relax and let go of any tension.

Take a moment to notice the natural rhythm of your breathing.

Bring to mind someone you respect and admire. This could be a historical figure, a loved one, or even a stranger who inspires you. Picture their face in your mind's eye and think about what it is about them that you find admirable.

Now, turn your attention inward and focus on your own sense of dignity. Imagine that you are surrounded by a bright, glowing light. This light represents your own inherent worth and value as a human being.

With each inhale, imagine that this light is growing stronger, filling your body with a sense of honored dignity. With each exhale, imagine that you are releasing any negative thoughts or beliefs about yourself that may be holding you back.

Take five to ten breaths on your own and then move through the rest of this practice.

Now, take a moment to appreciate your own worth and value as a human being. Recognize that you are deserving of love, and dignity, simply because you exist.

Connect this feeling to others. Come into the awareness that this same sense of dignity exists in every other human being on the planet.

Picture a world where every person's dignity is honored and compassion is extended, regardless of their biology, personality, and background. They too feel a sense of worthiness.

Take a moment to reflect on the ways in which you can promote dignity in the world around you. When you're ready, take a final deep breath in, and as you exhale, slowly come back to the present moment.

Know that you can return to this meditation at any time to reconnect with your own sense of dignity, and to renew your commitment to promoting dignity for all human beings.

An Exercise to Reflect on Our Common Humanity

Find a comfortable position, either sitting in an upright and dignified position or lying down flat on your back. Take a moment to settle into your body, allowing yourself to relax and let go of any tension. Notice the natural rhythm of your breathing without changing it.

Now imagine a vast web of interconnectedness spreading out across the world. Visualize this web connecting every person, regardless of their biology, personality, or background.

Make sure to see yourself as a part of this intricate network.

Reflect on the fact that every person, no matter their differences, shares the fundamental aspects of being human. Consider the universal experiences and emotions we all encounter, joy, sadness, love, fear, and hope.

Recognize that each person's life is a unique story and journey, but we are all connected by our shared humanity.

Now bring to mind a specific individual or group that you may perceive as different from yourself. It could be someone from a different culture, religion, or background. Hold them in your thoughts and recognize their inherent humanity, just like your own.

Contemplate the basic needs and desires that all humans share. We all yearn for love, acceptance, understanding, and fulfillment.

Consider the aspirations, dreams, and struggles that every person faces, regardless of their individual circumstances.

Reflect on the interconnectedness of our emotions. On how our happiness can inspire others, as well as our pain. Recognize that our shared capacity to feel and empathize binds us together.

Consider the strengths and virtues that are universally valued across cultures,
compassion, kindness, and resilience. Reflect on how cultivating these qualities within yourself can help foster connections and understanding with others.

Take a moment to explore any shifts in your perspective or a newfound appreciation for our shared humanity.

Think about practical ways you can honor and celebrate our common humanity in your daily life. This could involve engaging in acts of kindness, seeking opportunities to connect with people from different backgrounds.

Remember, this exercise is intended to deepen your awareness of our shared humanity and promote compassion and connection with others.

Visualization Activity to Raise Awareness of Our Common Humanity and Foster Unity Among Different Groups of People

Find a comfortable position, either sitting in an upright and dignified position or lying down flat on your back. Take a moment to settle into your body, allowing yourself to relax and let go of any tension.

Take a moment to notice the natural rhythm of your breathing.

Envision yourself standing in a vast open space, surrounded by people from different backgrounds, and cultures. Imagine a diverse group of individuals, each representing a unique part of humanity.

Now visualize a large, solid wall standing in the middle of this open space. This wall symbolizes the barriers, prejudices, and indignities that exist between people.

Take a moment to acknowledge any emotions that arise within you as you observe this wall. Allow yourself to feel the weight and impact of these barriers on individuals and communities.

Now, imagine a warm, radiant light emanating from within you. This light represents love, compassion, and understanding.
Visualize this radiant light expanding and growing brighter within you, enveloping your entire body.

Feel its warmth and positive energy spreading throughout your being.

As you continue to visualize, extend this radiant light beyond yourself, reaching out towards the wall. See the light gently permeating the wall, gradually dissolving it, and transforming it into a transparent barrier.

With each breath, imagine the wall crumbling further, revealing the faces and stories of the people on the other side. See their humanity, their hopes, their struggles, and their aspirations.

As the wall dissolves, visualize the individuals from different groups coming together, interacting, and forming connections.

Observe the barriers of indignity and prejudice being replaced by bridges of dignity, and compassion.

Take a few moments to bask in this image of unity and interconnectedness. Feel the sense of shared humanity and the removal of walls that once divided.

When you are ready, gently bring your awareness back to the present moment. Then reflect on the emotions and insights that arise from this visualization.

Consider how you can contribute to breaking down barriers in your own life and fostering a more empowering and dignified life and society.

Appendix C

Practices That Build Kindness and Compassion for Self and Others

The following section contains multiple practices that build kindness and compassion for self and others. Engaging in these practices helps develop the EHT attitude, Prioritizing Mindsets of Inquiry and Compassion. Explore all practices and return to the ones you find meaningful. This is not a comprehensive list as the number of possible practices is infinite. As you familiarize yourself with the practices named here, think about other possible practices that build kindness and compassion you can authentically engage in.

Thinking about the positive impact these practices have regarding brain health and well-being combined with the neuroplasticity principle of "we become what we practice", consider adding the practices you find meaningful into your habits and routines to create an empowering and dignified life.

Strategies For Incorporating Practices That Build Kindness and Compassion into Daily Habits

Start with Self-Kindness: Begin each day by showing kindness to yourself. Practice self-care, speak to yourself with compassion, and engage in activities that nurture your well-being. When you treat yourself kindly, you cultivate a mindset of kindness that can extend to others.

Practice Mindful Kindness: Be fully present in your interactions with others. Practice active listening, give your undivided attention, and show genuine interest in their well-being. Engage in acts of kindness with intention and mindfulness, savoring the positive impact you can make.

Small Acts of Kindness: Look for opportunities to perform small acts of kindness throughout the day. It could be holding the door for someone, offering a smile, sending a thoughtful message, or helping someone with a task. These small gestures can brighten someone's day and create a ripple effect of kindness.

Volunteer or Support Causes: Dedicate time to volunteer for a cause you care about or support organizations that work towards making a positive difference. Whether it's a local charity, environmental initiative, or community project, contributing your time and resources can have a significant impact.

Practice Gratitude: Cultivate a grateful mindset by regularly expressing gratitude. Take time each day to reflect on the things you appreciate and express gratitude to others. It could be through a gratitude journal, thank-you notes, or simply sharing your appreciation verbally.

Be Kind in Communication: Choose your words and tone carefully when communicating with others. Practice kindness in your conversations, both in person and online. Use words that uplift and support and avoid engaging in negative or hurtful dialogue.

Random Acts of Kindness: Engage in random acts of kindness by surprising others with unexpected gestures of goodwill. Pay for someone's meal, leave a kind note for a stranger, or help someone in need. These acts of kindness can create moments of joy and connection.

Kindness in Relationships: Nurture kindness in your relationships by being understanding, forgiving, and supportive. Practice active listening. Show appreciation and express love and kindness to your family, friends, and loved ones regularly.

Lead by Example: Be a role model of kindness in your community and inspire others to practice kindness.

Self-Compassion Exercise to Practice Kindness and Acceptance Toward Yourself When You Make Mistakes or Fall Short

Find a quiet and comfortable place where you won't be disturbed for a few minutes. Sit down and take a few deep breaths to center yourself.

Think about a recent mistake or experience where you may have fallen short of your own expectations.

Allow yourself to fully acknowledge the mistake without judgment.

Take a moment to offer yourself compassion for the mistake. Say something like,

"It's okay to make mistakes. Nobody is perfect, and it's natural to have areas where we struggle.
I am doing the best I can."

Think about how you can be kind and accepting toward yourself considering your mistake or coming up short. Maybe you can offer yourself encouragement and support, practice forgiveness, or show yourself some self-care.

Take a moment to acknowledge that being kind to yourself is an important aspect of self-care.

Say something like, "Being kind to myself is an act of self-compassion, and it's something that I deserve. It's okay to take care of myself and be gentle with myself, especially when I am struggling."

Place your hand over your heart and take a few deep breaths. Repeat the phrase,

"May I be kind and accepting toward myself, even when I make mistakes or fall short.

May I show myself the same kindness and compassion that I would show to a friend."

As you continue to breathe and repeat this phrase, allow yourself to feel a sense of self-love and acceptance. Visualize yourself surrounded by a warm, comforting light.

When you're ready, take one final deep breath and slowly open your eyes. Take this sense of self-compassion and acceptance with you as you navigate the ups and downs of life.

Remember that being kind to yourself is an ongoing practice, and it's something that you can cultivate over time.

An Inquiry Exercise That Encourages You to Put Yourself in Another Person's Shoes

Choose a person with whom you've recently had a disagreement or a misunderstanding. It could be a friend, family member, colleague, or even a stranger.

Take a few deep breaths to center yourself and clear your mind.

Imagine yourself in the other person's shoes. Visualize their thoughts, feelings, and experiences as if they were your own.

Try to understand where they are coming from and what may have led to disagreement or misunderstanding.

Take a moment to offer yourself compassion and understanding for any judgments or assumptions you may have made about the other person.

Say something like, "I acknowledge that my perspective may not be the only one, and it's important for me to consider the other person's point of view."

Think about how you would like to be treated if you were in the other person's position. What actions or words would help you feel heard, validated, and understood?

Take a moment to acknowledge the other person's humanity and inherent worth. Say something like,

"The other person is a human being just like me, with their own thoughts, feelings, and experiences. I want to treat them with dignity and compassion."

Place your hand over your heart and take a few deep breaths. Repeat the phrase,

"May I approach this situation with dignity and understanding. May I treat the other person with kindness and compassion, even if we disagree."

As you continue to breathe and repeat this phrase, allow yourself to feel a sense of connection with the other person. Visualize a bridge of understanding forming between the two of you.

When you're ready, take one final deep breath and slowly open your eyes. Take this sense of understanding with you as you navigate your interactions with others.

Remember that putting yourself in someone else's shoes is an ongoing practice, and it's something that you can cultivate over time.

Self-Compassion Exercise That Acknowledges Personal Limitations and Encourages You to Be Gentle with Yourself

Find a quiet and comfortable place where you won't be disturbed for a few minutes. Sit down and take a few deep breaths to center yourself.

Think about an area in your life where you feel you may have limitations, whether it's a skill, talent, or aspect of your personality. Acknowledge these limitations without judgment and accept that everyone has areas where they struggle or fall short.

Take a moment to offer yourself compassion for your limitations. Say something like, "It's okay to have limitations. Nobody is perfect, and it's natural to have areas where we struggle. I am doing the best I can."

Think about how you can be gentle with yourself considering your limitations. Maybe you can adjust your expectations, ask for help, or take a break when you need it.

Take a moment to acknowledge that being gentle with yourself is an important aspect of self-care. Say something like,

 "Being gentle with myself is an act of self-compassion, and it's something that I deserve. It's okay to take care of myself and be kind to myself, especially when I am struggling."

Place your hand over your heart and take a few deep breaths. Repeat the phrase,

"May I be gentle with myself in the face of my limitations.

May I show myself the same kindness and compassion that I would show to a friend."

As you continue to breathe and repeat this phrase, allow yourself to feel a sense of self-love and acceptance. Visualize yourself surrounded by a warm, comforting light.

When you're ready, take one final deep breath and slowly open your eyes. Take this sense of self-compassion and gentleness with you as you navigate the areas where you may have limitations.

Remember that being kind to yourself is an ongoing practice, and it's something that you can cultivate over time.

Perspective Mapping Exercise

Choose a Person: Select someone you would like to better understand and empathize with. It could be a friend, family member, colleague, or anyone you interact with regularly.

Draw the Perspective Map: Create a simple chart or use a large piece of paper divided into four quadrants. Label the quadrants as follows:

Says: Write down direct quotes or statements you've heard the person say.

Thinks: Speculate on the thoughts and beliefs the person may have based on their actions or words.

Feels: Identify the emotions or feelings the person may be experiencing in various situations.

Does: List the actions and behaviors the person typically engages in.

Gather Information: Spend time observing the person and engaging in conversations with them to collect information for each quadrant. Active listening and asking open-ended questions can be helpful.

Complete the Perspective Map: Fill in each quadrant with the information you've gathered. Take the time to reflect on what you've learned about the person and their experiences.

Reflect and Practice: Use the Perspective Map as a tool for reflection and practice. Put yourself in the person's shoes and try to see the world from their perspective. Imagine how they might be feeling or thinking in different situations.

Share and Validate: If appropriate, share your observations and understanding with the person. Validate their emotions and perspectives and let them know you are trying to empathize with them better.

Repeat with Different People: Practice the Perspective Map with various individuals to broaden your understanding of different perspectives.

This exercise helps build understanding by encouraging active listening, observation, and understanding of others' experiences. By seeing the world from someone else's point of view, we can cultivate greater compassion, and meaningful connections with others.

Active Listening Exercise

Actively listening to others involves paying attention to their words, tone, and body language without interrupting or becoming defensive.

To do this, focus on the speaker, maintain eye contact, and use nonverbal cues to show you are engaged. Repeat what the speaker has said to confirm understanding, ask open-ended questions, and avoid making assumptions or jumping to conclusions.

Speak Kindly and Compassionately: Speaking from a place of kindness and compassion involves using words and tones that show dignity, support, and understanding.

Avoid criticizing or judging others, and instead, use language that is supportive and encouraging. Try to put yourself in the other person's shoes and express your thoughts and feelings in a way that is honest and dignified.

Be Present and Mindful: Being present and mindful means being fully engaged in the present moment and focusing on the person you are interacting with. Avoid distractions, such as technology, and give the other person your undivided attention.

Notice your own thoughts and feelings without becoming overwhelmed by them and take a few deep breaths to center yourself and stay focused on the present moment.

Self-Compassion Exercise to Help Build Resilience

Find a quiet and comfortable place where you won't be disturbed for a few minutes. Sit down and take a few deep breaths to center yourself.

Think about a recent experience that was difficult or challenging for you. Maybe it was a mistake you made, a rejection you faced, or a setback you experienced.

Acknowledge the feelings that come up whether it's disappointment, frustration, or any other emotion.

Take a moment to offer yourself compassion for what you've been through. Say something like,

 "It's okay to make mistakes.
Everyone faces setbacks sometimes.
I'm doing the best I can."

Think about the ways in which you've shown resilience in the past. Maybe you've faced difficult situations before and come out stronger on the other side.

 Maybe you've demonstrated strength and perseverance in your personal or professional life.

Take a moment to acknowledge your past resilience and the strengths that have helped you get through tough times. Say something like,

"I've faced difficult situations before, and I've shown strength and resilience. I have the skills and tools to get through this."
Place your hand over your heart and take a few deep breaths. Repeat the phrase,

"May I continue to cultivate resilience and compassion for myself. May I recognize my own strength and resilience in the face of difficulty"

As you continue to breathe and repeat this phrase, allow yourself to feel a sense of empowerment and resilience.

Visualize yourself facing the difficult situation with strength and grace.

When you're ready, take one final deep breath and slowly open your eyes. Take this sense of resilience and self-compassion with you as you navigate the challenges and difficulties that may arise.

Remember, resilience is something that can be cultivated and strengthened over time. By acknowledging your own strength and offering yourself compassion, you can build the resilience you need to face difficult situations with confidence and grace.

Exercise To Learn More About the Perspectives and Experiences of Others

Identify a person or group of people whose perspectives and experiences you would like to learn more about.

This could be someone from a different cultural background, a different profession, or a different life experience.

Reach out to this person or group and express your interest in learning more about their perspectives and experiences. Ask if they would be willing to have a conversation with you, or if they can recommend any resources or materials that you could read or watch to learn more.

Approach the conversation with a spirit of openness and curiosity. Ask open-ended questions and listen attentively to their responses. Avoid making assumptions or judgments and be willing to consider new ideas and perspectives.

Look for common ground and areas of shared experience. Even if you come from different backgrounds or have different perspectives, there may be areas where you share common values or experiences.

Checking Assumptions Exercise

Reflect on a Belief or Assumption: Choose a specific belief or assumption that you hold. It could be about a person, a situation, a group, or a general concept. Take a few moments to think about it and write it down.

Identify Supporting Evidence: Write down the reasons or evidence that you believe supports your assumption. What experiences, information, or observations have contributed to the formation of this belief? Be honest with yourself and try to capture the key points that have influenced your thinking.

Question the Evidence: Now, take a step back and critically examine the evidence you listed in the previous step. Ask yourself the following questions:

"Are there any gaps or missing pieces in the evidence?"
"Are there alternative explanations or perspectives that could also be valid?"

"Are there any biases or assumptions present in the evidence that may have influenced your thinking?"

Seek Alternative Perspectives: Engage in an exercise of open-mindedness by deliberately seeking out alternative perspectives on the belief or assumption you identified. This could involve:

Researching opposing viewpoints or different cultural perspectives.

Engaging in conversations with individuals who hold different beliefs or perspectives.
Reading books, articles, or other sources that challenge your assumptions.

Challenge Your Assumption: Based on the new information and perspectives you've gathered, critically evaluate your original assumption. Ask yourself:

"Are there any flaws or weaknesses in your initial belief or assumption?"

"Has your perspective shifted or evolved considering the new information?"

"Are there elements of truth or validity in the alternative perspectives that you hadn't considered before?"

Reframe Your Assumption: Take the opportunity to reframe your assumption or belief based on the insights gained from this exercise. Consider adopting a more nuanced or open-minded stance, acknowledging that assumptions are not fixed but subject to change and growth.

Practice Awareness and Reflection: Moving forward, make a conscious effort to be aware of your assumptions in various situations. Regularly reflect on your beliefs, questioning their validity and considering alternative viewpoints. This ongoing practice will help you develop a more critical and open mindset.

Discuss and Share: If appropriate and comfortable, engage in a discussion or share your experience with a trusted friend, colleague, or mentor. Exploring assumptions together can deepen understanding and foster mutual growth.

Cultivating Curiosity Exercise

Recognize Judgmental Thoughts: Begin by becoming aware of your own judgmental thoughts. Pay attention to situations or individuals that trigger judgment or assumptions in your mind. It could be about someone's appearance, behavior, beliefs, or any other aspect that tends to evoke a judgmental response.

Pause and Take a Breath: Whenever you catch yourself engaging in judgmental thinking, pause for a moment and take a deep breath. This brief pause allows you to interrupt the automatic pattern of judgment and create space for a more mindful and curious response.

Shift to Inquiry Mode: Once you've taken a breath, consciously shift your mindset from judgment to inquiry. Replace judgmental thoughts with open-ended questions that promote curiosity. For example:

"What might be the reasons behind their behavior or choices?"
"What experiences or perspectives might have shaped their beliefs?"
"What additional information or context could I seek to better understand their point of view?"

Reflect on Assumptions: Reflect on the assumptions that underlie your judgmental thoughts. Ask yourself:

"What preconceived notions or biases might be influencing my judgment?"
"Are there any gaps in my understanding that contribute to my tendency to judge?"
"How might my own experiences or beliefs be shaping my perception of this situation or individual?"

Compassionate Perspective-Taking: Practice compassion by trying to see if there are possible elements of suffering. Imagine what their life might be like, the challenges they may face, or the experiences that have shaped them. Cultivate a genuine desire to understand their perspective rather than simply passing judgment.

Seek Understanding: Instead of jumping to conclusions, try to seek understanding through open communication or research. Engage in a conversation with the person you're tempted to judge, if appropriate and comfortable, or seek out diverse viewpoints through reading, listening to podcasts, or participating in discussions.

Challenge and Expand Your Views: Actively challenge your own beliefs and assumptions by exposing yourself to different perspectives. Engage with individuals who have different backgrounds, beliefs, or life experiences. Be open to questioning and expanding your own views, recognizing that there is value in diverse opinions and experiences.

Practice Gratitude and Compassion: Focus on recognizing the strengths, positive qualities, and shared humanity in individuals rather than fixating on judgments. Remind yourself that everyone is complex and multifaceted, deserving of understanding and compassion.

Journaling and Reflection: Incorporate journaling into your practice. Regularly reflect on your experiences, replacing judgmental thinking with curiosity. Write down any insights, challenges, or shifts in perspective that you've encountered. This reflection process can deepen your self-awareness and reinforce the habit of inquiry.

Embrace Continuous Learning: Approach life with a growth mindset, recognizing that you are on a journey of continuous learning and growth. Embrace the process of replacing judgment with curiosity as an ongoing practice and be patient and compassionate with yourself along the way.

By consistently engaging in this exercise, you can gradually shift your mindset from judgmental thinking to one of curiosity and inquiry.

Cultivating Compassion Exercise

Awareness of Judgment: Begin by bringing awareness to your own judgmental thoughts. Notice the moments when you find yourself passing judgment about yourself, others, or situations. Be gentle with yourself and acknowledge that judgment is a natural human tendency, but it can be transformed into compassion.

Pause and Breathe: When you catch yourself engaging in judgmental thoughts, pause for a moment and take a few deep breaths. Allow this pause to create space between the judgment and your response, giving yourself an opportunity to shift towards compassion.

Challenge Assumptions: Reflect on the assumptions that underlie your judgments. Ask yourself:

"What beliefs or biases might be influencing my judgments?"

"Are there any gaps in my understanding or limited perspectives contributing to my judgments?"
"How might my own insecurities or fears be affecting my perception of others?"

Practice Self-Compassion: Start cultivating compassion by directing it towards yourself. Acknowledge that you, too, are a flawed and vulnerable human being. Replace self-judgment with self-compassionate thoughts and actions. Treat yourself with kindness, understanding, and forgiveness, just as you would a dear friend

Cultivate Compassion: Shift your focus toward understanding others by cultivating compassion. When encountering someone's challenging behavior or situation, take a moment to imagine their perspective, experience and moments of suffering.

Consider the circumstances, emotions, and experiences that might have contributed to their actions. This empathetic lens helps foster compassion and reduces judgment.

Seek Common Humanity: Recognize the shared humanity that connects all individuals. Reflect on the fact that we all experience pain, joy, and the full range of emotions. Remind yourself that despite our differences, we all have basic needs, hopes, and dreams. This awareness helps dissolve barriers and promotes compassion.

Practice Loving-Kindness Meditation: Engage in a loving-kindness meditation practice to strengthen your compassionate mindset. Sit quietly, close your eyes, and offer phrases of loving kindness to yourself, others, and the world.

For example, "May I (or they) be happy, healthy, safe, and free from suffering."

This practice enhances feelings of compassion and connectedness.

Reflect on Interconnectedness: Reflect on the interconnected nature of all beings and the world around you. Contemplate how your actions and judgments impact others and the ripple effects they create. Recognize that cultivating compassion not only benefits individuals but also contributes to a more compassionate and harmonious society.

Extend Compassion in Actions: Take compassionate action in your daily life. Look for opportunities to be of service, lend a listening ear, or offer support to those in need. Practice small acts of kindness and generosity towards others without expecting anything in return.

Daily Reflection: Set aside a few minutes each day for reflection. Journal about your experiences, challenges, and insights as you cultivate a compassionate mindset. Celebrate moments of growth and self-compassion and note areas where you can continue to deepen your practice.

Patience and Persistence: Remember that cultivating compassion is a lifelong journey. Be patient with yourself as you navigate the ups and downs of shifting your mindset. Embrace the process of growth and continue to practice compassion, both towards yourself and others.

Exercise For Practicing Self-Care and Prioritizing Your Own Needs

Begin by finding a quiet and comfortable place where you won't be disturbed. Sit in a comfortable position with your eyes closed and take a few deep breaths to relax your body and mind.

Reflect on the different areas of your life that require your attention and energy, such as work, relationships, health, and personal interests. Consider how much time and effort you currently devote to each area, and how this allocation of resources makes you feel.

Identify one area of your life where you feel you could benefit from greater self-care and attention. It might be something like spending more time with friends, taking up a hobby, or engaging in regular exercise.

Set a realistic and achievable goal for yourself, such as scheduling a weekly coffee date with a friend, signing up for a painting class, or committing to daily yoga practice.

Create a plan for how you will prioritize this area of your life, and make sure to set aside time and resources to support your goal. Consider what steps you can take to create more space and time for this activity, such as delegating tasks or reorganizing your schedule.

Practice self-compassion and recognize that it is okay to prioritize your own needs and take time for self-care. Remember that taking care of yourself is not selfish, but rather a necessary part of being able to show up fully for others and live a fulfilling life.

Take action on your plan and make a commitment to yourself to prioritize your own needs in this area. Celebrate your progress and be kind to yourself, even if things don't always go as planned.

Repeat this exercise regularly and continue to identify areas of your life where you can benefit from greater self-care and attention. With practice, you can develop a greater sense of balance and well-being and live a more joyful and fulfilling life.

Exercise For Practicing Forgiveness and Letting Go of Grudges

Find a quiet and comfortable place where you won't be disturbed. Sit in a comfortable position with your eyes closed and take a few deep breaths to relax your body and mind.

Begin by bringing to mind a person who has hurt you in the past or a situation that has caused you pain or anger. Visualize this person or situation in your mind's eye and acknowledge the negative feelings that come up.

Reflect on the impact that holding onto this grudge or anger has had on your life. How has it affected your relationships, your sense of well-being, and your ability to move forward?

Acknowledge that forgiveness is a process and that it takes time to let go of negative feelings. However, recognize that holding onto anger and resentment only harms you, and that forgiveness can bring peace and healing.

Practice self-compassion by recognizing that it is normal to feel hurt or angry when someone has hurt you. Allow yourself to feel these emotions without judgment or criticism.

Repeat the phrase "I forgive you" silently to yourself, directing it toward the person who has hurt you or the situation that has caused you pain.

If it feels difficult to say these words, try saying them in your mind's eye or writing them down on a piece of paper.

Take a few deep breaths and imagine letting go of the negative emotions and feelings associated with the grudge or anger. Visualize these feelings leaving your body and mind and allow yourself to feel a sense of release and freedom.

Repeat this exercise regularly, as forgiving and letting go of grudges is a continuous process. With practice, you can develop a greater sense of inner peace, and improve your ability to navigate challenging situations with greater resilience and grace.

Remember, the key to this forgiveness exercise is to approach it with an open and compassionate heart, allowing yourself to let go of negative emotions and feelings, and cultivating a sense of peace and healing. By practicing forgiveness regularly, you can free yourself from the weight of grudges and negative emotions and live a more joyful and fulfilling life.

Exercise For Practicing Self-Acceptance and Self-Love

Start by finding a quiet and comfortable space where you can sit undisturbed.

Take a few deep breaths and allow yourself to relax.

Bring to mind a time when you felt proud of yourself, accomplished, or successful. This can be a big or small achievement, as long as it is something that made you feel good about yourself.

Hold this experience in your mind and allow yourself to feel the positive emotions that come with it. Let those feelings fill your body and mind.

Next, imagine a person you admire or respect. This could be someone you know personally, a public figure, or even a fictional character. Visualize this person in your mind and think about their positive qualities.

Now, imagine that this person is looking at you with love and acceptance. They see you for who you are and accept you fully, flaws and all.

Allow yourself to feel the love and acceptance coming from this person. Let it fill you up and imagine that it is healing any wounds or insecurities you may be carrying.

Self-Compassion Exercise for Going Through a Difficult Time

Find a quiet and comfortable place where you won't be disturbed for a few minutes. Sit down and take a few deep breaths to center yourself.

Think about the difficult time you're going through. Acknowledge the feelings that come up - whether it's sadness, frustration, anger, or any other emotion. Allow yourself to feel whatever you're feeling without judgment.

Now, imagine that you're talking to a close friend who is going through the same thing. What would you say to them? How would you offer them support and compassion?

Take a deep breath and imagine directing those same words of support and compassion to yourself. Say something like, "It's okay to feel the way you're feeling. You're doing the best you can. I'm here for you."

Place your hand over your heart and take a few deep breaths. Repeat the phrase,

"May I be kind to myself in this moment. May I offer myself the same love and compassion I would offer to a friend."

As you continue to breathe and repeat this phrase, allow yourself to feel a sense of warmth and kindness toward yourself. Visualize a comforting, supportive presence surrounding you.

When you're ready, take one final deep breath and slowly open your eyes. Take this sense of self-compassion and kindness with you as you navigate this difficult time.

Remember, practicing self-compassion is a process, and it can take time to cultivate. But the more you practice, the more you'll be able to show yourself the same love and kindness you offer to others.

Exercise To Notices and Disrupts Biases and Works to Challenge and Overcome Them

Start by acknowledging that everyone has biases, whether conscious or unconscious. Recognize that biases are a natural part of the human experience, but that we have the power to challenge and overcome them.

Practice self-awareness. Take time to reflect on your own biases and pay attention to situations where biases may be impacting your perceptions or actions.

Seek opportunities to learn more about different cultures, backgrounds, and perspectives. Read books, watch films, or attend events that expose you to new ideas and perspectives.

When you notice a bias, pause and take a step back. Acknowledge the bias and try to understand where it is coming from.

Challenge your bias by considering alternative perspectives. Try to put yourself in someone else's shoes and imagine how they might experience the situation differently.

Finally, take action to address biases in your daily life. Speak up when you hear biased comments or actions, and work to create a more empowering and dignified environment for everyone.

Curiosity Walk in Nature

Choose a Natural Setting: Find a nearby park, garden, forest, beach, or any natural environment that appeals to you. Ensure it is a place where you feel comfortable and can immerse yourself in the beauty of nature.

Prepare Mindfully: Before you embark on your nature walk, take a few moments to prepare mindfully. Take a few deep breaths, center yourself, and set the intention to approach this experience with curiosity and openness.

Engage Your Senses: As you begin your walk, consciously engage your senses. Take notice of the colors, shapes, and textures around you. Listen to the sounds of birds chirping, leaves rustling, or water flowing. Feel the sensations of the ground beneath your feet or the breeze against your skin. Smell the fragrances of flowers or the earthy scent of the forest. Allow your senses to fully immerse you in the present moment.

Curiosity Questions: As you explore, ask yourself curious questions about your surroundings.
Some examples include:
"What types of plants, animals, or insects do I see?"
"What do I know about them?"
"How does the sunlight filter through the trees or reflect on the water?"
"What patterns or shapes do I observe in nature?"
"How does the weather or season impact the landscape and its inhabitants?"
"What ecological interactions or relationships can I observe?"

Be a Nature Observer: Shift your attention from a goal-oriented mindset to that of an observer. Notice the intricate details, the interplay of elements, and the natural processes unfolding before you. Observe the behaviors of animals, the growth and transformation of plants, or the flow of water. Allow yourself to be captivated by the wonders of nature.

Follow Your Curiosity: If something catches your attention, follow your curiosity. Explore a fascinating tree, examine an insect or a flower, or investigate an interesting rock formation. Take your time and allow yourself to dive deeper into what piques your interest.

Reflect and Journal: Find a quiet spot in nature or sit on a bench to reflect on your experience. Take out a journal or notebook and write down your observations, thoughts, and feelings. Reflect on the connections you've made with nature and any insights or inspirations that arise.

Express Gratitude: Before concluding your nature walk, take a moment to express gratitude for the natural world around you.

Recognize the beauty, abundance, and interconnectedness of nature. Offer thanks for the opportunity to experience and learn from it.

Acknowledging A Moment of Suffering

Find a Quiet Space: Find a quiet and comfortable space where you can reflect without distractions. This can be a peaceful room in your home, a park, or any place where you feel calm and at ease.

Relax and Center Yourself: Take a few deep breaths to relax your body and mind. Allow yourself to become fully present in the moment, letting go of any tension or preoccupations.

Acknowledge Suffering: Bring to mind a moment of suffering that you or someone else has experienced recently. It could be a physical, emotional, or mental challenge, loss, disappointment, or any form of suffering that resonates with you.

Observe Your Feelings: Notice the emotions that arise as you recall this moment of suffering. Allow yourself to feel any discomfort, sadness, or suffering that may come up. Acknowledge that suffering is a part of the human experience and that it is natural to feel compassion towards those who are hurting.

Cultivate Self-Compassion: If you are reflecting on your own suffering, direct compassion towards yourself. Offer yourself kind and gentle words, acknowledging that pain and suffering are a normal part of life. Reflect on the shared humanity of suffering and remind yourself that you deserve compassion and understanding.

Cultivate Compassion for Others: If you are reflecting on someone else's suffering, extend compassion towards them. Put yourself in their shoes and imagine the challenges, pain, or difficulties they might be facing. Reflect on the interconnectedness of all beings and the shared experience of suffering. Offer kind thoughts and wishes for their well-being.

Loving-Kindness Meditation: Engage in a loving-kindness meditation focused on compassion. Close your eyes and repeat phrases such as:

May I (or they) be free from suffering.
May I (or they) find peace and healing.
May I (or they) be filled with compassion and kindness.

Extend Acts of Compassion: Consider practical ways to extend compassion and support to yourself or others who are suffering. It could be as simple as offering a listening ear, sending a supportive message, or performing a small act of kindness. Commit to acting and follow through with your intention.

A Meditation for Building Kindness and Compassion for Yourself and Others

Find a comfortable position, either sitting in an upright and dignified position or lying down flat on your back.

Take a moment to settle into your body, allowing yourself to relax and let go of any tension.

Soften the muscles in your face, relax the muscles in your shoulders, and feel your body relax from head to toe while following the full sensation of each breath as it enters and leaves your body.

Bring to mind someone you care about deeply, perhaps a close friend, family member, or mentor. Picture their face and imagine them standing in front of you.
Feel the love and warmth that you have for this person and allow it to fill your heart.

Now, bring your attention to yourself. Picture yourself standing in front of you,
offer yourself the same love and warmth that you feel for the other person.

Imagine sending yourself love, kindness, and compassion. Imagine holding yourself with the same regard, love and dignity that you would offer to a dear friend or family member.

Now, expand this sense of kindness and compassion beyond yourself and the other person. Bring to mind someone you feel neutral towards, someone you don't have strong feelings for or against.

Picture their face and imagine sending them love, kindness, and compassion.

Finally, see if you can bring this sense of kindness and compassion to someone whom you may have difficulty with. Maybe it's someone you may be holding onto anger or resentment towards.

Picture their face and imagine sending them love, kindness, and compassion, wishing them well, and offering forgiveness.

As you breathe, hold this sense of kindness and compassion in your heart, for yourself, and all people.

Allow it to fill you up and radiate out into the world, knowing that the more you practice kindness and compassion, the more it will grow and spread.

Take a few final deep breaths, feeling the relaxation and peace in your body and your mind.

Conclude this practice when you wish and then take a moment to appreciate the practice of building kindness and compassion and know that you can return to it whenever you like.

A Loving-Kindness Meditation

Find a comfortable position, either sitting in an upright and dignified position or lying down flat on your back.

Take a moment to settle into your body, allowing yourself to relax and let go of any tension. Soften the muscles in your face, relax your shoulders, and feel your body relax from head to toe.

Bring to mind a person who you love and care for deeply. It could be a family member, friend, or mentor. Visualize them in your mind's eye and feel the warmth and affection you have for them.

Recite the following phrases to this person out loud or silently:

> "May you be happy.
> May you be healthy.
> May you be safe.
> May you be peaceful."

> "May you be happy.
> May you be healthy.
> May you be safe.
> May you be peaceful."

Next, shift your focus to yourself.
Bring to mind your own image and silently or vocally recite the same phrases to yourself:

> "May I be happy.
> May I be healthy.
> May I be safe.

May I be peaceful."
"May I be happy.
May I be healthy.
May I be safe.
May I be peaceful."

Finally, expand your focus to include all living beings.
Silently or vocally recite the same phrases to all beings.

"May we all be happy.
May we all be healthy.
May we all be safe.
May we all be peaceful."

"May we all be happy.
May we all be healthy.
May we all be safe.
May we all be peaceful."

Remember, the key to this Loving-kindness practice is to approach it with a sense of openness and curiosity. Allow yourself to generate and receive feelings of love and kindness towards yourself and others throughout the days and weeks ahead.

Bibliography

McGilchrist, Iain. (2009). "The Master and His Emissary: The Divided Brain and the Making of the Western World." Yale University Press.

Siegel, Daniel J. (2012). "The Developing Mind: How Relationships and the Brain Interact to Shape Who We Are." Guilford Press.

Sapolsky, Robert M. (1998). "Why Zebras Don't Get Ulcers: An Updated Guide to Stress, Stress-Related Diseases, and Coping." W.H. Freeman.

Davidson, Ritchie, & Begley, Sharon. (2012). "The Emotional Life of Your Brain: How Its Unique Patterns Affect the Way You Think, Feel, and Live - and How You Can Change Them." Penguin Books.

Efferson, C., Lalive, R., & Fehr, E. (2008). The Coevolution of Cultural Groups and Ingroup Favoritism. Science, 321(5897), 1844–1849

Lazar, S. W., Kerr, C. E., et al. (2011). "Mindfulness practice leads to increases in regional brain gray matter density." Psychiatry Research: Neuroimaging, 191(1), 36-43.

Davidson, R. J., Kabat-Zinn, J., et al. (2003). "Alterations in brain and immune function produced by mindfulness meditation." Psychosomatic Medicine.

Lazar, S. W., Kerr, C. E., Wasserman, R. H., Gray, J. R., Greve, D. N., Treadway, M. T., ... & Fischl, B. (2005). "Meditation experience is associated with increased cortical thickness." Neuroreport, 16(17), 1893-1897.

Lazar, S. W., Bush, G., Gollub, R. L., Fricchione, G. L., Khalsa, G., & Benson, H. (2000). "Functional brain mapping of the relaxation response and meditation." Neuroreport, 11(7), 1581-1585.

Zimbardo, Philip. (2007). "The Lucifer Effect: Understanding How Good People Turn Evil." Random House.

Made in United States
Troutdale, OR
10/31/2023

14179219R00093